THE BOX
THE BUCKET SERIES BOOK FOUR

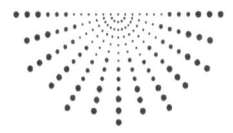

D.J. CATTRELL

This is a work of fiction. Names, characters, places and incidents either are the product of imagination or are used fictitiously. Any resemblance to actual persons, living or dead, events or locales, is entirely coincidental.

All rights reserved. Published in the United Kingdom by **Bad Cat Publishing**.

This book or any portion thereof may not be reproduced or used in any manner whatsoever without the express written permission of the publisher except for the use of brief quotations in a book review.

978-1-9196352-7-9

Bad Cat Publishing, JULY 2021
Copyright © 2021 D. J. Cattrell.

www.djcattrellauthor.com

Illustrations by Qi Fang

CHAPTER ONE

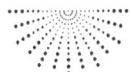

John woke slowly and rubbed the side of his face, it felt painfully warm, his head pounded as his vision began to un-blur itself. He looked around the floor of the valley to see Robins unmoving form laying on the ground a few feet from him. He started to remember what had just happened. Something had got in his head and it was horrible, like someone moving your arms and legs around without you wanting them to and talking for you without being able to control what you say.

He looked up through bleary eyes at the two suns, stood up slowly and then moved over towards Robin, but before he had taken three steps Clara also stood up and took a swipe at him. It was only out of surprise that he managed to avoid getting slapped again by her huge hand and he suddenly remembered why he had been lying on the ground. Clara had literally knocked whatever was in his head out of him with a punch to his cheek.

She went to take another swipe but John shouted out "No Clara please it wasn't me! I don't want to hurt Robin honestly" he rubbed his eyes and squinted.

Clara stood and thought to John. 'Boy try to kill Robin. Boy bad. Clara protect Robin.'

John's eyes widened and he said out loud, "Woah that is well weird. I can hear your thoughts!" He stopped talking and thought back to her, 'I know it looks like that Clara but something took my mind and I think you just knocked it out of my head so thank you.' Clara moved to stand between him and Robin. 'Please Clara I need to see if he's okay, will you please let me pass?' he thought to her.

Clara slowly stood back. 'Don't hurt Robin or Clara use 'punch' again'.

John nodded and moved slowly to Robin, rolled him over to see if he was breathing, thankfully he was. "Robin" he called out "Come on kid wake up mate."

Robin groaned and slowly opened his eyes, John helped him sit up being careful not to move too fast as Clara's rolled up fist was hovering above his head. Robin groaned, "You should have killed me" he said groggily "I've messed everything up and failed everyone. They're after Sarah not me and I'm here in this world, not there and I can't help her. What a self-obsessed arse I have been, kill me now!"

John looked up at Clara and raised an eyebrow, she in turn raised an earbrow and lowered her fist. "It's okay kid I have a new understanding of things. That weird creature may have taken my mind for a while but I think I know its weakness."

Robin looked up and breathed heavily before sighing, "Yeah, really, what's that then?" He sunk his face into his hands in self-loathing despondency.

John smiled and felt that for the first time in a while he actually had something to smile about. "When it takes you over it leaves its memories in your head." He sat down next to Robin.

Robin stared at John with a feeling of incomprehension mixed with bored indifference "What?"

John felt a bit smug. "Oh yeah and I can hear Clara Frab's thoughts as well! I'm beginning to understand this place a bit I think and I am loving it more and more, I just wish I had come here before!"

Robin slowly sat up straight. "You what!" he turned to Clara and put his hand out. She grasped his entire arm in one of her huge hands and pulled him up slowly.

John smiled looking up at Robin. "It left a whole lot of itself in my head and before you ask, there's no charge! These things are totally evil and there are hundreds of them. Dino's kill to eat and I know Dino's but these things are way older and seriously nasty, they cause pain for fun so they can feed off it, and…" he paused dramatically "I know their weakness!"

Robin stared at John "Well?" he blurted out "What is

their weakness?" then he turned to Clara "Thanks Clara by the way, are you okay? I lost you there for a while."

Clara thought back to them both 'Clara Frab worried, Clara Frab thought John Boy killed Robin.' She sat down into a half rock shape and waited.

Robin smiled at Clara then looked to John "Well genius, what are they scared of?" John looked at his two unlikely companions, "The Box being found, but then you knew that didn't you?" he said triumphantly.

Robin looked at John with some scorn, "No I didn't, I just guessed that was their weakness?" He looked at Clara who had sat down in the grass next to him, he could see that she was feeling exhausted.

John was a little excited "But you were right because that is their weakness, the Box being found, you guessed it right! I know it sounds crazy but whilst that thing was in my head, I got to take a look at it. When it first invaded my mind it just shunted my 'me', my consciousness out of the way and squatted in my head whilst it used my body as a puppeteer might use a puppet and at first, I was outraged and disgusted and felt violated by the intrusion, but then I stopped and noticed that I could look into the thoughts of this gross thing in my head. It didn't know, but I could read its thoughts and see its memories and so I calmed myself and took a good look around."

Robin wasn't up for this right now, he was as tired as Clara, he had failed everyone and just felt rubbish. "So?" he put his head back in his hands.

John sat down next to Robin and Clara and began to explain. "So, these things are ancient and evil and can flit in and out of other people's minds, which means they think that they are invincible. They are so arrogant, you just wouldn't believe how arrogant they are! They can get inside our heads and make us hurt each other, then they feed off our pain! They have been feeding off the pain that creatures in this world here have without them knowing it. Sort of like when someone breaks a bone, they lessen their pain a bit by feeding off of it but not enough that they get noticed, but they need the 'Box' to do that and that Box is how they jump in and out of minds and...." he took a stage moment of drama "...I know where it is!"

Robin was nonplussed "Yeah of course you do, how does that help?"

John grabbed Robin by the shoulders in some slight annoyance at his indifference as to what he was actually saying. "So, and this is the important bit, they all think at the same time like a hive of bees or ants or something, their minds are connected. It is the box that connects them all but if the box is ever opened then they can't connect any more no mind jumping, no telepathy nothing, they become just like us!"

Robin stared at John for a moment then assembled the facts in his mind, or tried to. "So, we have to find this box and open it? What happens if we manage to do that? Wait, Kobalos said 'Box have creature, creature have pain, Open

Box, kill monsters' maybe opening the box will kill all the monsters?"

John stopped for a moment. "That's where it all gets a bit hazy but this I do know, when I read their thoughts I could see, as real as you are sitting there, that you ain't the slayer that they are looking for, they are after your friend Sarah, they want her dead for killing one of them, the Esmer Alder, their 'Guardian' the one who protected the box. So, at the moment the box is unprotected!"

Robin looked sharply up at John, "I know, I don't know what to do to help her though, these creatures say they are in our world and hunting her. Mate, if they kill Sarah then they can have me for pudding because without her around my life wouldn't be worth living!"

John continued now that he had actually got Robin's attention, "They've hijacked the minds of the Dragons and half of them are chasing her down back in our world and half of them are here feeding on the pain that they can inflict on humans, dwarves and everything else that lives here."

Robin stared at John for a moment, soaking up what he had just said. "We have to get back there, we have to get back home!" he felt a rising panic, "I got it all wrong didn't I!" Then he shook his head "I told them I'd get it wrong but did they believe me? No. We've got to get back and save Sarah!"

John stood up and walked around thinking for a moment, "It's too late kid! I told you I saw their thoughts and they have found her home, and they're waiting for her there. If she turns up at her own home, they'll kill her for sure, they seem hell bent on revenge! I can't believe what I am about to say Kid but actually, we've got to stay here, we have got to find the Box and open it."

Robin jumped like he had just jolted like an electric daisy blast. "What? No! Don't be an idiot!" he stood and stepped back from John "Sarah is absolutely my priority now; I've got to go back to help her somehow. You don't know her; she is the best human being I've ever met!"

John shook his head, "There's only one way to help her now though, by stopping them from being able to mind jump and that means opening the Box. If you want to save Sarah then we have to find it. We can't fight them in our world because they can just hop from person to person or even animal to animal. We have got to destroy their ability to do that and then you will have a chance of saving Sarah."

Robin looked out at the valley they were in and back at John with some suspicion "So what are you saying? You want to stay here, in this world and help, how?"

John grinned mischievously back at Robin "Not sure, but some Kid told me a while ago to 'work with what I've got and not with what I think I should have!' After all this is huge. I don't want to go back to a world where those things rule us and they will for sure, if they get the chance. I know for sure, I felt their thoughts and that was their big mistake! We have to kill them here in this world, all of them, if you want to save your Sarah and our world. No question about it."

Robin just stared at him hearing his own words coming

back at him. "You can be such a smug git! Alright then," he said standing up, stretching and trying to think straight, he really hoped Sarah was okay, "so have you got a plan then?"

The moment was broken by the arrival of a very harassed looking Jasban, sporting a small and angry Dwarf known to the world and everyone as Dargal.

The Jasban slid to an undignified halt and tried shaking its antagonist off, but Dargal the Dwarf clung on and landed another blow with his small silver hammer onto the back of the Jasban. 'And that one is for the time you ate all of my square fruit crop and left us Dwarves hungry for a week!'

Dargal jumped off the Jasban and landed by the side of the fearsome beast, bringing his hammer down on the centre of the Jasban's left front paw. The Jasban squealed and drew back his foot and leaped sideways, as Dargal shouted out in his mind, 'And that one is for the time that you and your brother dug a hole outside of my cave and used it as a toilet! I might have been under the command of the Witch then but that was still a gross thing to do!'

The Jasban whimpered back 'That wasn't my idea and anyway we were just having fun!'

Dargal ignored the open-mouthed teenage humans and continued berating the Jasban even though one swipe of his armoured tail could have easily killed the Dwarf stone dead but wasn't in his nature. 'And if you ever try to wind me or my people up again by eating our crops, I shall kill you and roast you on an open spit Jasban, do I make myself absolutely clear? Actions have consequences!' The tiny but well armoured Dwarf drew his sword and pointed it at the Jasban.

In response the Jasban dropped to the ground exhausted 'Sorry, okay? We were just playing, we didn't mean any harm and…,' here he paused with a mischievous grin on his face as he thought back within thinking distance of the boys, 'The look on your face was precious when you came out of the cave and saw 'the toilet!'" and then the Jasban chortled in a gravelly squeaking sort of deep growl.

The Dwarf ran at the Jasban to attack him but Robin intervened quickly. "Dargal the Dwarf! You are Dargal aren't you? Sarah has told me all about you and how you are a great teacher!"

Dargal stopped dead in his track in some surprise and turned to Robin, "Yes boy, I am Dargal and this beast needs a beating!" This was such a peculiar sight to see a huge evil looking creature like the Jasban being told off by a creature no bigger than its own foot!

Robin looked at the Jasban who was clearly exhausted and continued to take Dargal's attention away from the poor beaten beast. "I am guessing that you are here to see us, so could you wait for a while before you give the Jasban his punishment, for whatever he has done?"

The Jasban padded over and dropped down next to Robin and thought to him, 'Thanks for the help there, Robin, don't think I could have lasted much longer, he is stronger than he looks and always grumpy! Everyone is safe now in that cave over there but they are exhausted. This 'Dargal Dwarf' wanted to see you.'

Robin stood and patted the Jasban's huge black furry shoulder. 'No worries Jasban and thanks.' Then he looked down at the impressively scary Dwarf, he was wearing his full battle armour and stood just above knee high. "Hello Dargal, um? How can we help you?"

The Jasban thought out the introduction to Robin 'You seem to know that the 'Dargal Dwarf' is an old friend of Sarah's and well everyone really. He and the other Dwarves were slaves to the witch for a while there until Sarah killed her…. it. You might think that he owes Sarah a bit and you might also think that he might say 'thank you' for me bringing him across the plain here to you.' The Jasban was still breathing heavily but recovering himself.

John's thoughts interrupted them 'How's the leg huge beastie thing, we saw you struggling there?'

The Jasban turned it snarly looking head towards John 'So, you can think now! I was wondering if you would ever talk properly, instead of using that squeaky noise you humans make. Leg's fine but I'm bushed. The Dragons seem to have lost interest then,' he thought out to them both. Looking around he continued, 'Never seen that many Dragons in one go before and all working together, that was weird and painful!'

Dargal dropped to one knee, looked up at Robin and spoke in a loud growly voice "You are the boy McRacker aren't you? Son of Jack McRacker?"

Robin looked down at this small yet formidable creature "Yes, my Dad is Jack McRacker."

The Dwarf stared at the ground between them "The Humans and my people give you our thanks for saving us from the Dragon fire. The Frab could not have protected us for much longer and you distracting the Dragons gave us just the few moments we needed to escape them. Thank you, Robin McRacker 'Dragon slayer.' You are truly like your father and already my people are telling stories of your heroic act."

Robin smiled at Dargal and shook his head "No problem Dargal. Sarah told me about you, she said that the witch's lair was behind your home, that the Witch had enslaved you for a long time but that you were okay now. Got to tell you though that everyone has it wrong about me being a Dragon slayer, it was an accident really."

Dargal paused and looked at John with a confused frown then back at Robin. "You went to kill a Dragon with a sword?"

Robin shook his head "Yes but…"

Dargal continued "And the dragon died by your sword?"

Robin furrowed his eyebrows "Yes but…"

Dargal swept his hand through the air. "Then you are indeed a 'Dragon slayer' then."

Robin sighed and his shoulders dropped. "Okay Dargal, I'm a Dragon slayer then."

John cut into the exchange. "Sorry Mr Dargal but the Witch was under your cave, wasn't she?"

Dargal turned his steel blue eyes up at John, his armour glinting in the sun looked suddenly threatening all by itself. "Who are you boy?"

John suddenly felt uneasy like he had gone to stroke a friendly looking dog that then bared his teeth at him. He looked at Robin then back at Dargal. "Um, no-one important really, well not here anyway?"

Dargal remained unimpressed. "Yes, her lair was there. Why is that important to you?"

John warmed to his subject. "Well she was a Guardian of these mind jumping creatures, wasn't she? The ones that are in the heads of the Dragon's at the moment I mean."

Dargal looked confused. "Yes why?"

John looked at Robin and smiled "That's where they are, the Alder, that's what they call themselves ain't it and she was the Esmer Alder wasn't she?"

Robin frowned. "What are you going on about?"

John threw his arms wide "She was a Guardian! What do you think she was guarding if not the Box! It's the box she was guarding that's why they are so pissed off with Sarah, she killed their protector of the box, the thing that gives them the ability to mind jump and now they are exposed, now they are truly vulnerable after thousands of years!"

Dargal drew his sword and pointed it up at John "How can you know this boy, are you a spy for these creatures?"

John thought it best not to mess with this diminutive white haired being of muscle and metal. "No, no!" he said excitedly, "I just had one of them in my head and I could see into its, or their minds. They think like a hive, they are all linked together. Can you show us the way to your cave please Mr Dargal? I'm sure that the Box is somewhere under there and I think that we might be at war with these 'Alder' creatures?"

Dargal looked at Robin. "Well McRacker, what do you think? Is the boy making sense, do you trust him?"

Robin looked at John. "Yeah, I think so. He says the Alder are trying to kill Sarah in our world and the only way to stop them is to destroy their box and kill the real 'them' here and I reckon he must be right."

Dargal took a moment looking at both boys and made a decision. "Then we must fight them together! My people owe Sarah our freedom and we will do anything to protect her and we all owe the McRacker's, for being our defenders throughout history. I will show you the way but we must go stealthily because if they know we are coming they will get into the minds of any creature in our path and try to kill us. If we are at war with these creatures then we will need weapons and we Dwarves know weapons!"

Robin knelt down next to Dargal and looked him in the eye. "Thank you Dargal, we are in your hands."

Dargal nodded and said out loud and up to the Jasban "You know where I used to live Jasban, can you carry us there through the tunnels, my people are licking their wounds and cannot help us this time?"

The Jasban had lain down and was slowly dropping off to sleep, his eyes now closed. Dargal poked him with his sword and he leapt up growling out in pain, 'What, ow! What did I miss?'

John thought out to him 'Dargal asked if you could get us all to his cave through the tunnels?'

The Jasban turned around and snarled down to the Dwarf whose sword was now sticking pin like out of the huge creature's rump. 'Yes, I can but if you stick me again, I'll eat you' he said looking directly into Dargal's eyes.

Dargal grinned, stood looking up at the growling Jasban and mischievously thought back. 'You're a vegetarian!'

The Jasban and the Dwarf were practically nose to snout. 'I can make an exception for you, little creature.'

Robin grabbed Dargal's sword and pulled it sharply out of the Jasban's rump who grunted in pain like being stung by a bee backwards. "We need to hurry so could you two try to get along?"

The Jasban almost harrumphed out loud. 'Climb on then but keep the Imp under control okay!'

Dargal growled back "I'm a Dwarf, you overgrown beetle!"

The boys looked at each other as they climbed onto the back of the Jasban and Robin pulled Dargal up. "Could we save the arguments until after we have found the Alder please?" Robin said weakly.

Dargal nodded. "I'll try but him and his brother used to torment us rotten when the witch had us under her spell!"

The Jasban thought up to Dargal. 'I have lost my brother Dwarf, I am alone.' Dargal frowned for a moment in understanding of the Jasban's loss. Dargal was old enough to have lost many friends and knew how hard that felt.

Dargal nodded in understanding at the Jasban's words then looked down at the beast he now rode and spoke out loud. "If we are at war Jasban then we may all lose friends and family. I will make a pact with you that if you are down, I will protect you, even though you don't deserve such protection!"

The Jasban snarled a smile and thought out loud back to the Dwarf so that all could hear 'Then I shall return the favour and watch out for you Dargal, as long as you promise not to stick me anymore!'

Robin made himself comfortable. "Don't touch his ears John, he doesn't like his ears being touched! Okay," John nodded, tried to find a way to climb onto the Jasban. "Clara?" Clara stretched out her arm allowing Robin to pull her up to join him and the others. 'You sure you can carry us all Jasban?'

The Jasban just grunted under the weight of four passengers and shifted his shoulders around. 'I can hardly feel you up there? Are you ready? Remember, no ears okay?'

Robin nodded. 'Okay, now let's see if we can find these Alder shall we, let's see if we can find this Box eh?' he thought out to everyone.

Without answering the Jasban turned and ran towards the hillside and into a wide cave with the boys, Clara and Dargal clinging on to his back as best as they could.

CHAPTER TWO

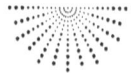

Sarah hugged the seemingly lifeless body of Kate whilst her mother tried to stem the flow of blood. She felt the furry tentacle of one of the Drask gently slip itself between them, then another and then a third. She looked behind her, through teary eyes, directly into the wide eyes of the gentle creature.

She felt the Drask tighten its grip around Kate's body and slowly lift her from Sarah' arms. More of its tentacles enveloping Kate as it raised her up. The other Drask joined the first and Kate disappeared in between the writhing bodies of the auburn-haired creatures.

Rachel knelt down and put her arm around her sister. Their mother hugged them both and said to her girls after a few moments, "I think she's gone. I am so sorry girls but when someone is gone, they are gone and we just have to think about how we loved them when they were here."

Sarah buried her face into her mother's embrace and sobbed as Rachel said, "It's not fair. If anybody should be dead it's him, it should be Drake." They all just sat for a while.

Jack walked over to Drake, picked up the gun and emptied the chamber of bullets onto the ground, then looked at the unconscious agent laying on the ground who was now bleeding from the punch he had received. "You won't be needing these anymore." Then threw the gun into the building behind them.

The Minister started to walk awkwardly away but stopped dead in his tracks at the deep warning growl of the Jasban. Jack looked over to him. "Don't let that human go anywhere Jasban, he has to account for all of this somehow."

Mr Jameson eventually said, "What are they doing exactly?"

Mary joined him and they both looked at the Drask with quite some curiosity. "Jack, come and see this."

Jack walked over to his wife and watched as the Drask began slipping their tentacles in and out of each other's grasps. Kate could barely be seen now. It was almost as if they had absorbed her into themselves and their tentacles moved faster and faster and then they started humming. "Not sure, maybe it's a death ritual, some creatures have them."

Aunty Tina and Mia joined the others and Aunty Tina said, "No I don't think so Jack, this doesn't remind me of anything I've seen before. Mary?" Mary shook her head just as the Drask stopped moving. Everyone stopped moving and looked at them. Even the Mudskippers from their temporary home on the tea trolley and the Cratalorg that had at last stopped its hissing joined in.

The hum became almost song-like, then that too stopped and like unravelling furry spaghetti the Drask slowly parted leaving Kate standing upright. Nobody moved and then after what seemed an eternity of expectation Kate gasped a breath into herself and stumbled backwards into the supportive tentacles of the Drask. Kate slowly opened her eyes that were now as purely auburn as the Drask fur in colour. Kate stood back up and took a step forward.

Sarah leapt to her feet and jumped over to Kate throwing her arms around her. "You're okay! You're alive!" Then she stepped back. "Are you okay?" She turned to her mother. "Is she okay?"

Kate smiled and croakily responded. "Yes, I think I'm okay, I feel dizzy though." She put her hand down to the wound in her chest that had now been replaced by just a small amount of glowing scar tissue. "Did somebody shoot me?" then answered her own question. "Yes, I feel it now!" She turned to The Drask and smiled, her voice soft and warm she said "Thank you!" She put her hands out and the Drask slipped their tentacles around them while purring gently.

She turned back to Sarah. "In my line of work 'Sarah the Adventurer' we make friends that we don't keep and never trust anyone but you are very different. Somehow I trust you and want to keep your friendship." She stepped forwards and hugged Sarah tightly.

Kate stopped moving and thought for a moment then said, "These creatures..." she paused and looked at the Drask, "These creatures are my saviours and will always be in my heart."

Jack beamed, "Well I for one am amazed and glad to see that you are not dead at all!" Kate smiled at him. "But what do we do now and what do we do with these two?" he said gesturing at The Minister who was still standing frozen in fear looking at the Jasban and Drake who still lay unconscious on the floor.

Mrs Jameson stood up. "Well" she said, "I vote for going home because if there really are Dragons heading for our place I shall want to know why and if they have done any damage, then I shall be having words! As for these two? Well Drakes no problem it seems and you" she said turning to the Minister, "You can come with us because if those Dragons are hungry, we'll have just the right meal for them!"

As usual she took charge of the situation. "Tina if you would drive the truck with Kate and Mia up front then the rest of us should just about be able to squeeze into the back. I hope the Drask don't mind sitting on the roof? Jasban if you would follow then we'll try to find a way of getting all you creatures behind back to where you belong."

Sarah looked to her mother "If it's okay mum I'll go with the Jasban. It'll be a bit like having White Tiger back for a bit." Then she turned to the Jasban. "That's if it's okay with you?"

Her mother nodded and the Jasban growled out a happy

thought to Sarah 'Jump up Sarah the Adventure' it'll be an honour.'

Drake started to gain consciousness and began to sit up. Just as he did so a Drask flung out a tentacle which smacked him full in the face with a powerful force and he fell back to the ground, unconscious again. The Drask then moved silently towards the Minister and it was somehow clear to everyone that they were not moving to him in a friendly way!

Jack grinned at Mia who was looking on open mouthed. "The Drask are amazing creatures for sure young Mia but don't ever annoy one!"

The Drask enveloped the Minister in their tentacles and moved towards the Truck. The Minister disappeared from the world with a muffled scream.

CHAPTER THREE

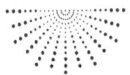

The Aide held Kobalos by the throat up against the wall of the Minotaur's cave, his face red with anger and frustration. Kobalos wriggled and tugged at his captor's hands and arms. The Aide shouted into the sprites face "You will show me how to get home or I shall tear off one of your limbs at a time until you do. I need to get out of here now. I need to share these 'feelings' with my brother. Tell me how to get back to my world, Now!"

Kobalos choked out his response, "Stupid Human can't control Stupid Human's 'feelings' Stupid male Human kill Kobalos before Kobalos help stupid human! Give gift to Minotaur!" Kobalos choked at the Human's stranglehold, his voice gurgled.

The Minotaur sat at his table. His grey dull eyes were fixed on the bucket that he was slowly crushing between his huge gnarly hands.

The Aide looked around the room and at the stone shelves upon which stood thirty or more of those little buckets. Flinging Kobalos against the opposite wall he shouted out, "If you won't help me sprite then I shall help myself!" With that he walked over and took down a small bucket from behind the Minotaur who just carried on his task unwavering.

Though Kobalos was tough from being a survivor of thousands of years of playing his cruel games and having fun being better than the stupid humans, his tiny body was what is was. He crumpled to the floor and spoke no more, his bright eyes dulled, then closed.

The Aide looked down at him and shouted "Well stupid sprite will you not try to stop me?" Kobalos just lay on the ground unmoving like a broken rag doll. The Aide stared down at the sprite and his emotions changed again as he just stared at the ancient creature that he had just crushed.

A few minutes passed as the Aide stood staring at the sprite. Then he looked at the small child sized bucket in his hand and his expression changed again. The red in his face turned pale and his eyebrows furrowed. He stared for a few moments trying to understand these emotions, this latest one being guilt. It was a horrible emotion and it consumed him, he had betrayed his new companion, and for what?

He stared down at the bucket and then his gaze turned back to the sprite, he dropped to his knees. Tears welled in his eyes and he slowly and carefully put down the portal then shouted out. "What have I become!" Tears started to fall from his reddened eyes falling heavily onto the floor.

The Aides breath blew cold in the Minotaur's cave and after a while of wrestling with his mind, he made his decision. A final and inescapable decision, he gathered himself together, wiping the new wetness from his eyes. He stood, walked to the Minotaur and put his hand on the impossibly huge beast's shoulder then leaned in to look the Minotaur in the face and said "Take this burden of emotions from me Minotaur, please free me from them, take 'the gift' from me, please!" He then exhaled that gift that he had carried from the Unicorn, he exhaled the blue misty cloud directly into the Minotaur's face and stood back.

The Minotaur breathed in and his eyes filled with a red mist of anger! His muscles filled again and bulged, he stood up slowly, gripped his workbench in the huge and ornately decorated cavern that was his home within his Labyrinth of tunnels. He snorted a dark steam from his nostrils, his eyes flamed crimson and then flashed blue, the blue of the Unicorn, he looked around his home and he looked down at the crushed portals lying around the floor and he snorted with rage.

He looked at the inert form Kobalos lying on the floor of his cavern, his oldest irritation and yet his oldest friend and his shoulders burned in anger. He breathed in deeply again and his whole being filled with pity and rage and then after a dangerous pause, he let out a deafening roar. The sound of his pain filled the entirety of his cave, the Labyrinth of tunnels and beyond.

The sound echoed around the ancient caves and the

tunnels that had been carved out millennia before by Dwarves. Dwarves of ages long since gone, grandfathers even to Dargal as well as those carved out by the Minotaur himself who was old enough to have seen those other ancient creatures pass from this world.

The Labyrinth of tunnels around them shook and the creatures within them crouched in fear. The Minotaur was back and he was angry, really angry! The Aide sighed out his last emotions and they were relief to lose, then he looked down at the sprite and knew sorrow, a lasting sorrow that he would always remember but not feel and a gladness that he had spared his brother the burden of these 'emotions'.

The Minotaur stood to his full height and spoke out to no one and everyone. "Wherever you creatures are who took my mind from me, know that I am angry. I will find you and I will kill each and every one of you that I find." Then he stomped over to the Aide, towering above him, his eyes flashing burning red with anger but with sparkles of blue shining out. "Pick up the Sprite and follow me Human, I mean to go to the Dwarvian Armoury and you will help me kill these monsters!"

The Aide looked at the Minotaur with no expression and said calmly. "I shall do as you ask and help you because I know now that it is right to do so. I have had emotions and I understand what you feel, but know that I have none of the emotions you are experiencing right now and so I have no fear of you or the monsters."

The Minotaur turned to this unusual Human and growled

out. "I had lost my passion, if that is what you are like I pity you, but you brought me back to myself and for that I am eternally grateful so you have no need to fear me. Will you help me help Kobalos, I need to take him back to his home, back to his people."

The Aide looked up at the Minotaur "You have emotions so I would pity you as well if I could feel pity. Yes, I shall help you because I have now felt pain and guilt and they are horrible emotions. Revenge is destructive but it is a useful tool against such a cruel enemy that took your emotions from you." With that remark he picked up Kobalos and cradled him in his arms. "He is breathing, we may find help somewhere along the way."

The Minotaur snorted small flames and strode out of his workshop towards the Dwarvian Armoury growling.

The Aide followed with Kobalos' limp body clutched to his chest. He felt nothing and yet had the memory of 'feeling' which was perhaps worse, he was also experiencing a new thing that was not a feeling, it was a sense of purpose. Saving Kobalos was his purpose. A sense of purpose, a direction and it was good. He had somewhere to go, he had purpose. He had Kobalos.

CHAPTER FOUR

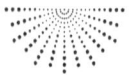

Robin held onto the Jasban's raised scales as it raced through the darkness of the tunnels. John had taken to clinging on to Robin around his waist as the beast thundered along. "How can he see where he is going?" shouted John into Robin's ear.

Robin shouted back "I have no idea, I can't see anything!" He turned slightly "I just hope he doesn't trip because at this speed we'd end up like pancakes against some wall! Having said that though, what a rush!"

John couldn't quite believe what he had just heard "What a rush!" he mimicked "What a rush? We might die and this is a rush to you? You really are as mad as you dad!"

Robin laughed out loud "Maybe I am. He lived here with Sarah for years in this mad world and they are both crazy!" his shout out reverberated into the passing wind "This place changes you."

The Jasban began to slow down as he came to a tunnel that became a cave, which became an ornate hall with steel glinting all around that appeared to be partially lit by gleaming stones.

As the Jasban slowed to a walk John asked "How can it be light down here? It feels like we are so far underground." The Jasban stopped and everyone including Clara slid off his back and looked at the hall before them.

Dargal jabbed Robin from behind with a bony finger "This boy, is a Dwarf shaft, this leads to the tunnels around and beneath my home and to the lair of the Witch and the caves beneath her lair. Before you ask, no, we didn't know we were building our homes above a nightmare!"

Robin smarted from the jab "I didn't say anything!"

Dargal looked at the boys with a challenge in his eyes but as both said nothing he carried on after an uncomfortable pause. "These stones are called 'Speardrops'. they have their own light and we use them when tunnelling. We're not far from the cave where she laid for so long Robin, in fact we are close to the surface and my cave. We are in," and here Dargal paused and swelled with some pride, "We are in the Dwarvian Armoury!"

John looked down at the stones ignoring the weaponry of war around him and concentrating only on the stones. "These are an amazing light source! If we could take these back home, we could make life easier for, for…." John struggled to think for a moment.

Robin completed his sentence "For a cost? For money eh John? For a few quid?"

John looked at Robin for a moment assembling what he had just said "Right, just right. You want to do this now then let's do this!"

Robin looked over at John "What? Am I wrong eh, you don't think that this is worth a few quid? You can't make a profit from this then? I've got £300 in my back pocket that says that you want to make a few quid out of this. Am I wrong eh? Am I?"

John stared at Robin in disbelief "What!" he walked around the floor of the cave for a moment, Clara looked on with some uncertainty. "Is that what you think? You think I just want to line my own pockets, is that what you think? To make money out of all of this for myself, is that what you think?"

Robin walked around the Jasban, a bit taken aback by John's outburst. "Well yes, of course I do because money is all you talk about isn't it? 'John the Ingenious'?"

John put his hand up to Robin and continued walking around the hall eventually saying, "Yes! Yes, I do want to make money and do you know why? Do you know why they call me 'John the Ingenious?' It's because I can make a lot of money but why do they call me that do you think? Do you know why I like to make a lot of money?"

Robin was feeling a little defensive now. "No idea, why?"

John rose himself up to his full height of self-indignation whilst the other creatures watched the confrontation with some surprise. "Because I am good at raising funds for charities, you, halfwit! I don't keep a penny of what I make, it all goes to charities, mainly to the homeless!"

There was a very cringy uncomfortable silence in the cave for quite a few cringy moments whilst Robin stared at John in some disbelief and his body sort of crawled with cringy embarrassment at what he had just heard, then for a few moments Robin looked down at the ground and just said, "Oh! Right, um, right then, sorry." then he exploded a bit, "Well why didn't you say so in the first place? You let me believe that you were a greedy money grabbing toe rag, why didn't you just say you were a charity worker in the first place? Why eh, why?"

Clara felt the tension in the air but it wasn't anything that she understood so she curled herself up into a rock shape and waited, and uncomfortably thought out to everyone in the room, 'What are Homeless?'

John stood his ground but looked at Clara. "People who don't have a home, a place to be safe, I help them to be safe."

Clara nodded and looked at John with a new eye. 'Clara lose home before, Clara feel not safe when this began. John good man, Clara like John more now.'

John felt a warm glow in his mind from Clara and smiled at her. "Thanks Clara, means a lot!"

Robin though was still angry "This is just theatre to you ain't it? You could have told me from the get go that you were a charity worker so why didn't you eh?"

John squared up to Robin again. "Well because you were

such a self-righteous git frankly!" he leaned towards Robin as they faced each other barely an inch apart. "You had your mind made up about me from the get go didn't you? You just knew I was a baddun didn't yer eh? Eh?"

Robin smarted from the truth of John's words and spat back. "Well that's how you painted yourself isn't it, demanding money from me for a passage to here? And another thing, you..." but his words were cut off from a sharp pain in his buttocks as Dargal slapped a wooden stick with a tiny barb in it into Robin's butt, Robin yelped out in pain!

Dargal continued from where he had left off 'This' as I was saying,' he looked at the Jasban with a frustrated pause and thought a private thought to him. 'Bloody human teenagers!' Then continued throwing open his arms to encompass the whole cave. 'This is the Dwarvian armoury and yes, we have made weapons for creatures of your size as well as us 'normal sized people.' Look around and choose something that you think might help you defend yourselves.' Dargal looked at the Jasban again and thought to him 'Are they always like this?'

The Jasban smiled a snarl down to the Dwarf and thought back to him privately 'Humans chatter on without saying anything, but to be fair they are always ready to play.'

The boys looked at each other and then around themselves and sure enough they were now in a cave that gleamed with light that also glinted off metal, a lot of metal. Robin looked over to see a trebuchet. "Blimey Dargal was that my Dads? He talked about using something like that."

Dargal smiled "Yes lad, one of my best weapons of war that one was. I had to make it really sturdy though knowing how carless your Dad was with weapons. He used it twice, once on a Cratalorg invasion and once to rescue you. On both occasions, I had to rescue it and repair it, although where the other two are that I made for him remains a mystery! Three of these beauties I made and only one remains. If you ever get home ask him where he lost the other two because he wouldn't tell me!"

Robin looked down at Dargal. "Um, okay? I'll try to remember?"

Dargal continued his speech. "Your Dad is a brilliant strategist but lacks a love of weapons, he calls them 'functional' but to me," and here Dargal walked up to the trebuchet and stroked it, "these weapons are an artistic thing of beauty!" This is a Trebuchet, a sort of catapult but this beauty could hurl fifty Frow into the future it is so strong! Just look at the tension in that spring!" The boys looked over at the huge catapult, it clearly was a thing of beauty. It had what looked like stories carved into every beam of it that reminded them both of tapestries that they had seen at school. The polished woodwork that made up most of the weapon also had silver filigree winding decoratively along it. It truly was beautiful.

Dargal continued "How can you lose something this big, not once but twice? And this one I had to rescue from the

Dragon's lair after your Dad left. He may be brilliant but he is also bloody careless!"

Robin looked down at Dargal. "You should see what he did to my football shirt! He is my Dad but he drives me nuts."

Dargal nodded in understanding back at Robin.

John looked around at the store of weapons that was bigger than any warehouse that he had ever been in. There was every conceivable weapon, in every size to suit from a giant to a mouse. The weapons were hanging or had been placed on shelves that surrounded the massive cave. "Wow Dargal, this place is amazing!"

Dargal smiled. "Yes, it is, and it is centuries old. Look to the left of you and take a sword or two. Take whatever weapons you can carry on you that keeps your hands free."

John looked at Robin. "Ok but why do our hands need to be free?"

Dargal shook his head. "Because if we are going to fight then you had better be ready."

John shook his head. "I hadn't planned on doing any actual fighting, I thought we could just get to the box, y'know, sneak in and grab it!"

Robin looked back at Dargal as he picked up a sword. "Last time I held one of these I accidentally killed a Dragon."

John looked dumbly at the armoury. "I've never had a fight before, not even in the playground."

Dargal was beginning to lose his temper. "You can't go into a fight unarmed! Grab some weapons NOW!"

Then a noise from across the cave drew their attention. They turned around to see a creature twice the size of any Human accidentally knock over a rack of hammers with one of its slowly drifting tentacles. The hammers clattered to the stone floor filling the quiet of the cave with a loud clanging sound.

The creature had arms and legs like a human but with its knees on backwards and barbed claws adorning its hands and feet. From its back and sides, swaying muscular tentacles weaved slowly back and forth, like it was considering its next move, they moved like a thought in motion. Its eyes were a mix of purple and pure black and they almost filled its oval head. The boys stood transfixed and stared at the sight before them for a moment. The beast had wide nostrils and a tiny cruel spikey toothed mouth; its dark fur glistened against the Dwarvian lights.

Dargal pushed a sword into John's hand, which he looked down at in surprise. "If it comes at you swing this around a lot and hopefully you won't die!"

John whispered. "It's one of them, it's an Alder but I don't think it can mind jump without leaving itself vulnerable, they have to go into a trance I think, to be able to do that. It will have to fight all of us in its own form."

Robin looked down at Dargal. "These things Dargal, these are real, these are the things going after Sarah?"

Dargal didn't take his eyes off of the Alder whilst saying, "Yes boy, these are the Alder, they are what the witch was protecting, she was their Queen and their Guardian for thousands of years and when Sarah killed the Witch they started very slowly waking up from their hibernation." Robin looked back at the Alder with a sense of fascinated horror.

The troupe just stood staring at the creature who, in turn, stood staring back with its tentacles swaying menacingly behind it, it looked very much like it was weighing up its chances against them.

Robin slowly raised his sword as did John and Dargal, preparing themselves for whatever might happen next. Clara stood slowly to her full height next to Robin and the Jasban grinned wildly, getting ready to use his teeth and claws even though this creature was as big as he was. The Alder looked back at them, paused and then slowly retreated out of the cave.

The boys looked at each other and Robin's pupils were wide with surprise and astonishment. "That's what they look like? They're huge and those eyes!"

Dargal smiled. "Looks like it was too scared to actually fight us though." And swung his tiny sword in a triumphant circle above his head.

Both boys looked down at this proud metal-covered Dwarf who stood maybe just over knee high tall to them and they marvelled at Dargal's comment. That creature could surely kill them all in a moment, except maybe for the Jasban.

Then gradually the far end of the cave started to turn dark as twelve huge tentacled Alder pushed their way into the enormous cave. Their feet slapping down on the floor and the tentacles on their backs searching out the air for any taste of fear as they knocked over more racks and tables sending metal weapons flying across the floor of the cave. The Alder stopped briefly, fifty metres or so from the troupe and then growled a low thrum of a growl turning their misshapen heads towards Robin and his friends.

Dargal stopped swinging his sword and said, "Oh, oh dear!" The boys lowered their swords and even the Jasban took a step backwards.

CHAPTER FIVE

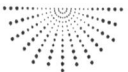

The road home had been filled with the incredulous stares of the people they passed. They gasped in amazement as the Jasban strode through roads and lanes thronging with onlookers. More and more people lined the roadside as word of the impossible group of people and alien creatures reached ahead of them. By the time the truck eventually reached the village, just outside the town of Colchester, the streets were teeming with onlookers.

This was truly a sight to behold, even in the fading light of day, which was being made lighter by the burning buildings surrounding them and yet at the same time darker because of the black smoke rising off them that hung in the sky above.

An enormous army truck being driven by an odd looking colourful old lady, with the most unbelievable couple of beautiful furry octopus type Orangutan coloured creatures riding on top of it. Following on behind the truck was the most fearsome and impossibly giant armoured looking alien panther, but it was way scarier looking. Someone in the crowd whispered in awe as they passed by "It's the Devils cat!" Nothing like this had ever been seen in the history of mankind and to add to the scene the panther was being ridden by a teenage girl who looked to all the world, like she was riding a gentle giant pony across a buttercup meadow!

Right now, though nothing could have been more confusing for the Jasban as he stared around at the people staring back at him and whispering among themselves, he thought up to Sarah. 'That's a valley full of humans Sarah, why are they staring at us like that?'

Sarah smiled a thought down to her old friend as they loped along the road and under the bridge that led to her village. 'This is new thing for them Jasban. They have never seen creatures like you or the Drask before and they will be surprised and maybe a little bit scared. New stuff scares humans, I think. This will be the first time in their lives that they have seen Dragons and you look a bit like a Dragon without wings. Roll with it for now and let's see what's ahead.'

What was ahead and above was chaos. The road into the village was festooned with army and police vehicles, fire engines flashed their blue lights all around and large tents had been erected all along the main street. The villagers were looking up in fear, watching the Dragons flying around in the smoky air as they belched out their fire, seemingly taking great pleasure in setting alight anything and everything they could!

The Jasban tried smiling at some of the humans who were gathered in the car park of the 'Half Keg', the local village pub, but they just cringed and stepped back in horror, fear and amazement. Sarah noticed and thought down 'Try not to smile Jasban, to them it looks like you are aiming to eat them.'

Tina pulled the truck to a slow halt at the barbed wired fences that adorned the entrance to the street where the McRacker's and the Jameson's lived. They were immediately surrounded by a throng of soldiers, police, firemen and ambulance crew all calling out questions. "Are you Sarah the Adventurer?" and "Are you here to stop this?" and "Are you a part of this, what's going on, can you stop it?"

The only person not in a uniform was Commander Grayson and he strode out from behind the uniformed mass, looked at the terrifying beast with the young girl perched atop and shouted out above the noise "Young lady, are you the one who is called 'Sarah the adventurer'?"

Sarah looked down from the impressive height of the Jasban and asked somewhat suspiciously "Depends who's asking?"

Grayson looked around at the impossible scene before him. "My name is Commander Grayson and I'm the head of all armed forces in this country. Young lady we have a situation here, you seem to be the key to that situation and by the look of the beast that you are riding it seems to me that you have some understanding of what is going on here. There are creatures occupying the minds of Dragons and they want you dead because you killed one of them. Does that ring any bells with you? And what exactly is that thing that you are riding? It looks like a horse from hell!"

More Dragons continued arriving and joined the mass circling overhead. There was now a new more urgent screeching to their cacophony. Mrs and Mr Jameson climbed out of the back of the truck followed by the others, Jack helping Rachel lift down the 'Tea trolley of infinite surprises', as it had now become known to the Mudskippers. They walked round to join Sarah (the humans that is, not the Mudskippers, that would be impossible!)

The Drask seemed content to stay atop the truck entwining their furry tentacles with each other and sitting upon something that was wriggling in a futile attempt to free itself and making 'harrumphing' noises. Mary tugged hard at the beetley Cratalorg who in turn was pulling away from her like a dog afraid of ghosts. Mary shouted up to Sarah. "Check out the Cratalorg's eyes Sarah. Either 'The Esmeralda' is still alive or there's something like her around here!"

Sarah saw the unmistakable stone-grey eyes of one that had been enslaved by 'The Esmeralda' but that was impossible! Sarah had killed that vile creature, she turned to Grayson, her mind racing and coming to a terrifying conclusion. "You said there is something occupying the Dragons minds, what do you mean?" Then she remembered herself and shouted down to Grayson. "Sorry, he's a Jasban and a vegetarian, I know he looks a bit scary but he's very friendly really."

Grayson was careful not to get too close to the beast nonetheless. The Jasban smiled in greeting and everyone around, including Grayson, took a cautious step back. "I'll take your word for that Sarah. Whatever is in the minds of those Dragons can jump into anyone of us at any time, I could fight Dragons with my soldiers and our weapons but these mind jumping creatures have us flummoxed! If we try to kill a dragon, they just leave the mind of it and jump into one of us then they turn our own weapons against us. They have already destroyed most of our weapons by getting our own men to break them!"

Jack looked up at Sarah. "I knew there had to be more like the Esmeralda in the other place! There's always two or more of everything, from the look of this there were a lot more like her back there."

Grayson cut in. "That's not the worst of it I'm afraid" he looked down the street at the chaos of burning houses trashed vehicle, the smashed street furniture and the circling throng of Dragons in the air still spewing out their fire. "They want us to give you to them by midnight or they say they will start killing us all. I don't doubt for one moment that they could."

Kate appeared from the truck and walked forwards to stand beside Sarah, the Jasban and the families. "That won't be happening Commander" she said calmly, "I know what those creatures are, they are vile and evil, they can't be trusted but they will not be taking Sarah, Sarah is under my protection."

Grayson was surprised. "Kate! Your boss should be taking care of this, where is he and what makes you so sure you can stop me from handing Sarah over?"

Kate looked at Sarah and nodded reassuringly to her but spoke to Grayson. "'Regi' is no longer my boss. I resigned from my post and I resigned from the service because the world has changed for us all, particularly for me. When this is over Regi will be facing kidnapping charges and more, along with Drake. This, Commander, is what makes me sure that you will not be handing Sarah over."

She looked at an overturned tank at the top of the burning street, then back at Grayson and waved her left hand almost nonchalantly, Grayson's eyes followed hers.

The tank righted itself and turned its guns upwards towards the Dragon filled sky, Kate then narrowed her eyes and swept her hand sharply upwards. The guns fired and within seconds a shell exploded right in the centre of the airborne Dragons. They briefly scattered only to quickly regroup and turn their attention in Kate's direction. "I have had my eyes opened by this sixteen-year-old girl and I know what is important to me and what is not now. The creatures controlling these Dragons want a fight so let's give it to them!"

Grayson looked visibly impressed. "This has been the strangest few days I've ever known Kate, truly, but even if you can do what you just did, how can you stop those mind jumping creatures from making us kill ourselves? We have no defences against that happening."

Kate walked towards Grayson and looked at the swarm of Dragons, Dragons sat on the roofs of the houses that hadn't already been burned to the ground while those still in the skies reigned down fire and terror. Kate nodded more to herself than Grayson. "I am your defence now so believe in me, or don't!" Then as one, the sitting Dragons took to the air to join the others like a cloud of fear in an approaching storm and turned their wrath towards her.

The Jasban turned around to face the onslaught and Sarah shouted over to them both. "We have another hope left apart from Kate. We have Robin. We have to hope that he's alive and that whatever he has been doing in 'The other place' will help. Our last hope is Robin!"

Then Grayson's worst fears became a reality, his eyes turned jet black and his voice changed to a rasp as an Alder took over his mind and control of his body. "At last you have come to us 'Slayer' when you die balance will be restored! You robbed us of 'The Guardian', we can still smell her blood on your skin, for her death you must die, then we can find a new Guardian." The soldier's eyes changed to jet black as they and the Commander turned in unison towards Sarah, Kate and the others, all intent on getting to Sarah.

Kate put herself between Sarah and the Alder. "That won't be happening today parasite!"

The puppet that was now Grayson turned to Kate in surprise. "She was you! You were a host of our Queen!"

Kate walked straight up to Grayson without fear. "I had her in my head yes and I know you lot are not as powerful as she was. Yes, she was your Queen, wasn't she? Just like bees have a Queen, but you lot are just drones, all be it highly evolved drones, but you were just her drones and you need Sarah to die so one of you can step up to take the Queen's place. You might be able to get in and out of minds but you have no magic. Not like the Guardian did, not like the Esmer, the Queen, not until one of you steps up!"

The Commander smiled. "You can't stop us from taking the slayer human, we can smell the blood of our Queen on her skin, stand aside or die and know this, wherever she goes we will find her, we have her scent now and we are all powerful!"

Kate looked back at the families and then back at the Commander. "No, you are not, you are weak and scared. If I ever come to your world then you should fear me because the Esmer was in me and I know you, parasite and I know where you really are. You live under the Esmer's Lair, don't you?"

Then Kate screwed up her eyes and put her fingers to her temples then opened her eyes wide in some shock. "I have her memories Alder, you have been hiding from the world and living in fear of being found, you fear the box being found and...." Kate paused and searched through the Witch's memories in her head, she dropped to her knees and put her fingers to her temples then shouted out, "You are scared that I might know about 'The Box', aren't you!"

Kate looked at Sarah and projected an image into her

mind. Sarah's pupils widened as her eyes filled with tears. "Well I have found you and I know about the box and how cruel you really are!" Kate looked absolutely shocked at a memory that she had just found. 'The Box' was a prison and a cruel prison at that, it was the box that gave 'The Alder' the ability to mind jump.

She turned to Sarah whilst ignoring the threat in front of her. "The Alders' weakness is 'The Box' in the other world, I have found in the witches' memories in my mind, they show me that the Alder are cruel beyond belief! We need to free the creature from the box."

She turned back to face the creature controlling Grayson. "We are coming for you Alder, Sarah the adventurer, Rachel the Intrepid and I are coming for you. I am coming to free that poor creature in the box and when we do you will feel the pain that you have fed off of for so many millennia and we will kill you all!"

The Commander or at least the creature controlling him moved forward. "You do not believe that we can destroy you do you human? Then die along with the Slayer, you cannot stop us from killing her and your knowledge will die with you, we are untouchable!"

All of the Dragons in the air stopped for a brief second and then just flapped their wings like a swimmer would tread water in a panic as the Alder left their minds and all of the humans within twenty feet of Grayson and beyond turned to Sarah with their now 'jet black eyes', paused and then ran at Kate, Sarah and the Jasban. All of them picked up weapons as they approached. The Alder would have their revenge on the Slayer!

Jack looked at the people running to attack them all and shouted out. "We all have to stand to protect Sarah now! Try not to hurt these people too much, they are a bit possessed and not quite themselves just now. Having said that..." a small older lady then jumped to punch Jack on her way to get to Sarah. "Don't hold back!" and he grabbed the older lady by the hair and swung her weight against herself sending her spinning off hitting a dark-eyed younger man who was approaching from the other side of Jack, this sent the pair of them tumbling off down the pavement is a mass of tangled arms and legs.

Sarah looked at the chaos all around her as everyone tried to protect her from her 'possessed' neighbours and friends. Jack was doing his best to hold back three people without hurting them too much, but was finding he had to throw out the occasional kick and punch. Her parents were holding down two of their neighbours in strangle holds on the ground and apologising to them at the same time, after all they were normally good neighbours, when their minds hadn't been taken over by the Alder.

The Drask were using their tentacles to spin their attackers back away from Sarah, having let the Minister fall from their grasp off the top of the van, where they had held him captive. He had hit the ground, feet first luckily, but had then crumpled down in a heap, dazed and confused.

Aunty Tina and Scruff were working together trying to

push people back away from Sarah. Aunty Tina started by jumping on them, which was like having a curtain shop of fabrics drop on you from a great height and then the pair of them trying to squash the attackers into the pavement.

Mary had taken control of the truck and was reversing it back and forwards to block off more of the would-be attackers and revving the engine furiously as a threat.

The Jasban was doing a great job of just squashing people without actually killing any one and the Mudskippers were shouting their encouragement from the tea trolley, which, having survived being knocked about quite a bit over the last few hours, was now looking somewhat battered!

Kate was waving her arms back then forwards, using her powers to send various attackers flying off to the sides of the road. Sarah grabbed at her arm and shouted over the mayhem. "This won't work, they are after me and they won't stop until they have killed me. Until that happens everyone here are likely to get really badly hurt or even killed!"

Kate looked at Sarah whilst sweeping a few more attackers away from their attach of them. "Then we have to get you away from here girl, but I just can't work out how to do that! What I do know is that I will not let anything happen to you Sarah, I will not let any creature in this world or any other hurt you! You are the one person in this world that I feel any real connection to now and I need to hold onto that, onto you."

Rachel heard this and nearly exploded as she breathlessly exclaimed. "That's it, that's it, I know how to stop this, well, at least for a while." She looked at everything going on. "We have to go back to the 'Other Place' Sarah. That is the only way of getting you out of here!" and with that she untied 'The Bucket' from her belt. "They will follow us and everyone here will be saved!" But no one paid much attention to her, so much was happening right now that everyone was just in defence mode.

No one that is, apart from Mia. On hearing Rachels statement Mia looked slowly around at the chaos, as the tumblers of logic in her mind started falling into place, solving the puzzle that she was facing. She barely noticed the cloud of black-eyed Dragons flying around over the village belching out their fire at anything that wasn't already burning, nor the decimated buildings now empty and wrecked. These were only a small part of the equations running through her head.

She watched clouds of smoke drifting in the air from scorched trees, roasted tiny birds, blackened flora and fauna, even a blackened and crispy looking massive spider with wings that looked entirely out of place. There were soldiers, firemen and policemen trying to help people away from the devastation of the village. Suddenly those tumblers in her mind all fell into place, like a slot machine hitting the jackpot. It was as if a light went on in her head, she suddenly understood everything that was happening here and now. Here and now was real! Only one option, only one 'equation' was possible.

She ran over to the girls "Rachel is right!" she shouted "Rachel is right, because in all probable scenarios no one here can win, we can only protect Sarah. But if there is a place that Sarah can go to then she might be able to get the Dragons and the creepy mind jumpy monster things to follow her, thus having a much higher statistical probability of saving this world. From what Rachel and Sarah have told me, Sarah is better off fighting the mind jumping creepy monsters on her own turf, in the world that I used to think they had made up, but appears to be, beyond all probability, real!"

Kate frowned at Mia. "What did she just say?"

Sarah smiled at Mia then looked back to Kate. "She said I should be the bait that takes the Dragons and 'The Alder' back to the other place. Thanks Mia, I think you are right. Rachel, you are a genius just like Mia!"

Mia beamed a smile at her friend Rachel and then shouted out to her. "That is if you can keep the portal open long enough for them to follow you back there. Can you do that?"

Rachel looked at the others. "I'm pretty sure I can but who knows right now? I need to concentrate, forget everything that is happening right here, right now. Sarah, hold the bucket with me."

Sarah looked at Kate who nodded and said, "If she can get you out of here then she can save all of us, at least for now, do it, go back there, to 'The Other Place', if you can. I can give you some space to do that, just give me a few seconds." Kate dropped to one knee and drew back her hands, concentrated hard, then drew her arms wide and shouted out. "Cover your ears, NOW!"

The families stopped what they were doing for a moment and looked at Kate with her arms held wide out. "Trust me, cover your ears!" Everyone got the message, stopped fighting off their attackers and put their hands up to their ears just as Kate swung her arms together and made the loudest clap that had ever been heard in this world, one that was a tsunami of a sound wave even greater than a group of clapping Frab could produce.

A sonic boom burst out from that clap, causing every human and every creature to drop for a moment, instinctively covering their ears and stiffening their muscles. Even the Dragons in the air reeled backwards. When the people eventually stood, their eyes had returned to normal and the mind controlling creatures had been shaken out of their heads, for now at least! Kate turned to Rachel. "We have only minutes before the Alder get back into people's minds Rachel so open your portal quickly."

Rachel paused and looked around, it was true, all of the fighting had stopped and people were standing around looking at each other with much confusion. Rachel looked back at Kate. "If all of these Dragons could get through to here then the portals must be open all the time. Maybe, just maybe we really can get the Jasban and the others back to their home as well?" she said as the Jasban grinned and drooled with hope, he really did miss his brother.

Sarah nodded. "That would be amazing Rach if we could, wouldn't it?" She looked at Jack, then at the Jasban and the Drask.

Jack nodded whilst helping Mr and Mrs Wainwright, from number 52, to get back to their feet, he had been holding them down on the ground not minutes ago, trying to stop them from attacking Sarah. "Worth a try I'd say. When you press the jewels Rachel just try thinking of the creatures here and think of them there that might help!"

Rachel nodded, put her thumb on one side of the bucket while Sarah put her thumb on the other side and the sisters looked into each other's eyes. Despite the seriousness of the situation and the worry of their parents both girls grinned at each other, this was them truly together for the first time in forever!

Rachel's mind drifted just for a nanosecond back to the first time she had used the bucket and then pressed the jewels in hard. Smoke billowed out of it and within the smoke five Unicorns burst out into the here and now and Rachel looked up at the full-sized, very real Unicorns surrounding her in utter surprise. A shimmer emanated from Brian and the world around the families seemed to slow down around them as if they were in a bubble, like Flings. Grayson and everyone else outside of that circle seemed to be moving in slow motion.

Brian looked down as he swirled around out of the smoke, his hooves hitting the ground as he trotted down to halt in front of her. 'You thought me here Rachel which can only be fate because we need you now and Sarah and anyone that can help! They don't know it but Robin and John need you, I feel it so keenly that it almost hurts, so climb on quickly! Our world is about to be decimated in a way we have never seen before and we need all of the help we can get.' His thoughts were urgent in her mind.

Jack burst out, "Robin's alive! Did you hear that Mary? He's alive!" Mary threw her arms around Jack and let the tears fall from her eyes in a mix of exhaustion and elation.

Rachel was stunned momentarily but then asked. 'Can we bring the others back with us Brian, they need to get home.' Then she looked at Kate, 'and Kate, she can help too.'

Brian thought back to her. 'Anyone who can help right now will be welcome Rachel.' He trotted around Sarah and Rachel and addressed the Jasban. 'I am glad to see you; old friend, your brother will be very glad to see you but I must tell you that he is hurting right now. He has been fighting Dragons and creatures I have never seen before to protect others.'

The Jasban turned his mind to Brian. 'He is alive?' He asked.

Brian whinnied. 'Yes, I share the thoughts of all the creatures my friend and their thoughts show me your brother is proving to be a strong friend to Robin!'

The Jasban grinned and drooled with pride for his little brother. 'Of course he is, he is Jasban!'.

Brian continued, 'The Griffins are hurt.' At that simple statement all the eyes of the families turned to Brian in shock. 'I no longer hear their thoughts and so I have no idea of how to fight these creatures that Robin and John face' The Griffins were the unseen law of 'The Other Place', how could they be hurt?

Rachel looked through the chaos. "Kate will you come back to the other place with us? Going back is the only way we can save everyone here and you can help!"

Kate stepped forward and looked at the scene before her. The Jameson's were recovering from the sonic boom as were everyone else human or otherwise. Next, she did something that she had not done for what felt like a very long time, she smiled and looked at Rachel. "Would I have the privilege of riding a real Unicorn?" Kate's face was a picture of hope. "That has always been an impossible dream of mine because up until a few seconds ago I knew they didn't exist, even as a child and if we are going into some sort of battle then I would really like to just feel good about at least one thing before we do."

Rachel looked at Kate confused. "I think so," and then asked Brian 'Does she?'

The Jasban rose and let two people up whom he had been holding down. 'A small hero though? My little brother… really?'

Brian looked at Kate and whinnied back to Rachel. 'Yes, now hurry before everyone comes to their senses!' Then turned back to the Jasban. 'I am not sure, I think so, time to come home friend but only to face a battle with creatures that have remained hidden for millennia. They are the personification of evil, we may not live through this, they are rising and they seem to be unstoppable!'

Kate smiled a quiet smile, she had faced the 'Unstoppable' before and had manged to, if not stop it, then at least to change its direction. Out of some sort of instinct she looked at the other four Unicorns, bowed her head, knowing somehow that she must ask for permission.

A Stallion walked from behind the other three and breathed a blue mist over her. She looked up and upon hearing it in her mind say, 'I feel you are different from other Humans as you have changed recently, I hope we can be friends?'

Kate lifted her head, smiled and thought out, 'May I?' The Unicorn lowered himself to one knee and Kate put her hand on his mane, took a grip and then jumped lightly onto the back of the Unicorn. 'I hope so too, my name is Kate,' and stroked his silken mane.

The Unicorn stood and walked in a slow circle 'Kate, does that name have a meaning?'

Kate shook her head at the Irony of what she was about to think. 'It means 'pure of heart' but I have been a Government agent and am far from pure!'

The Unicorn warmed in her mind and replied. 'Our actions don't always match our intentions. My name is 'Conquester' and I have done terrible things in my long life, but always for the greater good. I carry a shame and a love in my heart for everything and everyone in equal measure and I feel that you are the same.'

Kate's eyes welled up at this statement. He had described her exactly, she could have cried at that moment but managed, just, to supress a welling of more tears of his understanding of her. He then nailed her immediate love for him by saying. 'When we forgive ourselves for that, then can we give more of the loving parts of ourselves to others, can't we Kate!'

Kate leaned down and hugged her new friends' neck and nuzzled into his mane and said nothing, she didn't have to. For the first time in her life she felt like she had a complete soulmate and a warmth spread through her from head-to-toe.

Sarah jumped up onto to Brian's back and shouted to The Jasban. 'Will you take my little sister old friend?'

The Jasban thought back to them both 'My pleasure and if we can kill whatever hurt my brother then so much the better! You ready Rach? Jump up little one.'

Rachel put her foot on the Jasban's knee and jumped up onto his back still clutching her bucket then thought out to the Drask and the Cratalorg. 'Get in close because I only have one chance at getting you all home right now, sorry Mudskippers but you're going to have to stay here for now and help protect this world.'

At the mention of such an important task the Mudskippers stood in their makeshift tea trolley pond and thought back. 'We will fight to the last for the 'Nose shovelling saviour' and we will not be found wanting!'

Mrs Jameson then ran over to Rachel and Sarah. "Girls wait!" she shouted, "You can't go Sarah, I lost you for eight years I don't want to lose you again!"

Sarah looked down at her Mother. "I'm sorry Mum but you know I have to go. I am probably the only one who can stop all of this because all of this is really my fault, if it can be stopped at all that is. I promise you that I will try to stop it all and do my best to get back to you as soon as I can. If I can't then I won't let anything happen to Rachel, I absolutely promise mum."

Mrs Jameson put her hand up to clutch Sarah's. "This is your third time back there Sarah, whatever is happening now this is your third time back there and you have to make your choice to stay there forever, or to come home, will you come home?"

Sarah looked down at her mum and across to Rachel then over to Jack and Mary. "I can't honestly say Mum; White Tiger has gone and yet that world might still need me. I can't make that choice now, at least not until I can escape from the crazy stuff that's happening and think more clearly." Then she leant down to her mum. "Wherever I am I will always love you and Dad, you are just the best parents any crazy girl like me could ever have!" then she rose up and grabbed onto Brian's mane still looking her mother in the eye.

Mrs Jameson looked back at her husband who just shook his head in despair and shouted back. "I don't think that we have a choice Debbie, we have to let the girls go and do whatever they can do." Mr Jameson very rarely used his wife's actual name in front of anyone just because everyone had always called her Mrs Jameson, even Mr Jameson, but this was a time like no other.

Debbie looked up at her girls with tears in her eyes. "You make sure to keep each other safe and come back home the moment you can understand?" the girls nodded. "I mean it!" she said.

Sarah put her hand down and clasped her Mother's again. "I hope I can mum and if not, I will make sure that Rachel comes home." They let go of each other, knowing that there was a very real possibility they may never see each other again. They looked at each other with understanding that this was breaking each other's hearts, but also that there was no choice to be made right now.

Sarah thought out to Brian. 'Let's go Brian and I want to know who hurt the Jasban because they are going to be first on my list, followed by these creatures who are the cause of all of this, they are all going to die!'

Mia shouted out from behind everyone. "I don't exactly know where you are going and I have no maths to back this up, but I believe you have a fairly good chance of coming back because of what and who you are!"

Rachel responded in an equally loud voice. "Thanks Mia, look after our 'mad' Aunt, will you?" Mia looked up at Aunty Tina and smiled a little weakly. Aunty Tina just rolled her eyes, smiled and put her arm around Mia.

Jack then looked over to Sarah. "If you see Robin tell him I got the idea now and I'm sorry about his football shirt...." he paused for a moment, "And I love him! Oh, and thank him for not being dead, if he is not dead!"

Sarah frowned back and then smiled. "Course I will Jack and by the way..."

Jack looked at her expectantly. "Yes?"

Sarah smiled. "I have already won this one!" Jack just shook his head and laughed. "Get to the Ravine girl, the traps are set, you'll be safest there won't you? Go home Sarah." He said this with more feeling than anyone there understood. Sarah nodded and smiled, she was going home, she was going to her real home, 'Sarah the Adventurer' was going back to their Ravine.

Kate gripped her knees hard against the sides of her new friend and shouted. "Grayson, when they come at us can you slow them down? They won't be 'mind jumping' if they want to follow us and we really need a head start."

Grayson thought for a moment. "We'll do what we can Kate. Just make sure that this world of ours isn't compromised again!" Kate nodded back.

Brian began to trot then canter around as Sarah shouted out to Kate. "Was it true what you said just then Kate? Do you really know where they are, the real them?"

Kate was following on her Unicorn and replied. "Yes, I do, they are under the Witch's lair hiding like snakes hiding under a rock. There are hundreds of them and they don't even belong in that alien world, they are an infestation that needs to be exterminated!"

"Do you think we can beat them Kate?" Sarah's words were full of uncertainty.

Kate smiled back as Conquester, her Unicorn friend, drew neck and neck with Brian and the Jasban. "With these friends, your skills, your intrepid sister and me with whatever magic I have, I think we have a chance at least!"

"Then you must hear and understand this Kate that the world that I grew up in is very different from this one and not everything you see will be real".

"Oh, I get that now Sarah, you are in charge now and I shall help how I can."

Then Sarah looked to Rachel who nodded. "I'm up for this Sis, let's end once and for all, I just want to come back home with you and a have a 'normal' life!"

Sarah then looked up to the skies thinking out as loud as she could threw out her challenge to the creatures. 'Hey! You up there, you Alder monsters, I am the slayer of your mad Queen and I'm going back to your world so if you want a fight and kill me then come and get me you slimebags!"

The Alder heard the challenge loud and clear through the minds of the Dragons. All of the airborne reptiles' heads turned towards her, the other Dragons leapt into the air from the broken and crushed houses where they were perched to join the others in their quest to reach 'The Slayer'. Then Sarah shouted out "Stand back everyone and let them follow us, Rachel we need to go!"

Rachel nodded, closed her eyes and concentrated hard, the smoke surrounding them began to swirl into a circle faster and faster until it became a huge vortex.

Brian galloped into the air and with the others following shouted into all of their minds. 'Be prepared everyone, we could be going into a new form of hell!' With that he leapt back into the smoke quickly followed by the other Unicorns, Jasban, Drask and finally the hissing Cratalorg.

The Dragons began their descent and tried to follow them swooping down in their hundreds from all around the village. This time Grayson was ready and rattled off commands into his walkie talkie. New soldiers appeared seemingly from out of no-where and began firing at the Dragons from the ground with reserve weapons. The Dragons initially reeled back away from the smoke and hail of bullets in utter surprise.

Jack whooped in delight and turned to Mary. "See Mary, always have a backup plan! This will give the girls a few more minutes at least!"

The Dragons screeched, circling the village in the air for several minutes, belching out fire in pain and annoyance. The reprieve didn't last long unfortunately. They re-grouped in the sky and began to drop down towards the fading smoke of the portal with determination. It was as if they didn't care about how badly they would get hurt.

Grayson realised that these 'mind controlling' monsters didn't care if the Dragons they were occupying were injured or killed. So, as they began their descent, he ordered a cease-fire after all the Dragons were not the real enemy here. That girl and her friends needed time so he shouted a new order as a vast torrent of water flew up from the ground at the Dragons as Grayson released the water cannons sending the Dragons spinning once again, spluttering and trying to regain control. He managed this manoeuvre twice more until his eyes turned black as an Alder took his mind. The Alder in Grayson dropped the walkie talkie from his hand and crushed it underfoot, the Dragons now had nothing holding them back and began to fly into the vortex. They seemed to get smaller and smaller in the smoke as if they were travelling a huge distance in a few seconds.

At last Grayson's eye returned to normal as he shook his head and shivered, and breathed in deeply. With his mind now free from the control of the Alder he watched the last Dragon leave his world and shouted out to the remaining members of the families. "They're gone, what do we do next?"

Mrs Jameson turned and saw Regi being picked up off the ground by a suited man that she had grown to like a lot. The Aide, still sporting dark glasses, was holding his former employer by the back of his jacket as if holding something that smelt very bad. "Well you can arrest him for Treason and attempted murder for a start!"

Grayson smiled. "With pleasure Madam!" and ordered several soldiers to arrest Regi. "And then?"

The Aide released his grip and Regi slumped back down to the ground burbling incoherently. The soldiers picked up the prisoner under the arms, dragging him along with feet dragging along the ground behind him. The Aide wiped his hands down his jacket as if he had held a skunk's bottom for a moment. His face though showed little emotion as he turned to Mrs Jameson "He has stolen my brother from me".

Mrs Jameson scowled back. "We will find a way of getting him back somehow." The Aide tried a smile as he knew that it was a proper response but his face looked more like he had just eaten a bee.

Mrs Jameson looked out at the devastation before her and turned back to Grayson. "Well after you have agreed to rebuild our village, then you can listen to us when we try to help you understand that this is not the only world?"

Grayson nodded to this his new teacher. "I am all ears Madam! We are all ears as a Government and as a nation. I have to ask you if you would consider being an Ambassador between our worlds, if and when the time comes for that."

Mrs Jameson looked at the wreckage that was her street concentrating now on her destroyed home. "If my girls survive this and come home then yes. I think you know that if that happens then this world owes its existence to my two daughters."

Grayson nodded "I believe that to be an irrefutable truth Mrs Jameson."

Debbie sighed and turned to Mr Jameson. "It's done, we just have to hope now." Her words rang from the past into her ears as the ring of smoke disappeared into itself, she turned to her husband and said "Here we go again!"

CHAPTER SIX

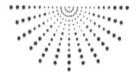

Dargal whispered to the boys without taking his eyes from the silent enemy that faced them from across the Armoury. "We are going to walk backwards verrrry slowly boys, as we go you are going to pick up anything that feels like a weapon and bring it with you okay?" Then he thought out to the Jasban. 'I am taking them through the stores caves but you will be too big to fit through the entrance. When I shout, I want you to turn and run past three openings in the tunnel directly behind us as fast as you can, turn left at the fourth and it will lead you up to the floor of the creek, do you understand?'

Each of the creatures stood as tall as the Jasban himself and he was in no doubt that they could be a match for even him. 'You're in charge now Dargal, you won't have to tell me twice.' The Jasban thought back looking at the creatures slowly advancing along the floor and walls towards them. The Jasban never felt fear except when White Tiger was around but right now, right now he felt fear.

Dargal spoke slowly and calmly to the boys. "Let's go boys, no sudden movements okay and when I say run then run as fast as you ever have okay?" Both boys nodded and started walking slowly backwards stretching their arms out to slowly pick up anything that felt heavy or sharp or spikey. Neither of the boys took their eyes of the creatures coming towards them but their hearts pounded in their chests. They both knew without a doubt that, even though he was small, the Dwarf was totally in charge here.

Robin whispered to John. "Have you seen their eyes, it's like they are boring into me!" His hand ran over a Dwarvian mace, then he felt a human sized swinging axe which he picked up and slowly hooked onto his belt.

John answered in the same whisper. "I think that we need to get away from these things really quickly, there's no profit in us being dead!" His hand felt a large knife in a leather sheath and he slid it into the front of his shirt.

. . .

The Alder began quickening their pace towards Robin and the others. Dargal thought to them both as well as to Clara, who had returned to her rock shape some feet behind them. 'To the door everyone but only move slightly quicker than they are moving.'

CHAPTER SEVEN

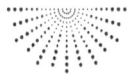

This time no one 'emerged slowly' from the smoke, they came galloping out at full tilt and hit the ground running from the terror of the mind taken Dragons that were definitely chasing not far behind them.

Brian was pretty sure that they had a good head start from that Bevy of dangerous flying oversized reptiles. If they could all reach the woods in time that might afford them some time to hide, but it wouldn't give them long, they all knew that the Dragons would burn down anything in their path to get to Sarah and kill her. But if they could reach the woods at least that would give them some time to plan their next move!

Unfortunately, as they burst forth from the stone circle, they surprised two more 'Alder infested' Dragons. The creatures leapt into the air from their perch on the top of the monolithic stones where they had been waiting patiently for just this possibility. They immediately began chasing after the group, screeching out their frustration of having missed their assigned targets as they came through the portal!

Everything was a rush as the troupe galloped from the ancient stone circle, all hoping that they would have enough time to get to cover before the Dragons could catch up with them. The Drask were slowly overtaking them all and seeming to fly just off the ground with their tentacles whirring as they glided through the air, still as graceful and as swift as sparrows, but two Dragons were sweeping down out of the skies and the chase was on, immediate and intense. Being caught up by those two monsters would be the quick end of them all.

The Cratalorg leaped off of the Jasban and ran into the distance. Whilst it hated everything that had happened to it and everyone who had been a part of that, it was now free and had its mind back. It ran away from everyone so that it could hate more creatures and felt good about that. For the Cratalorg this was a strange feeling, a new feeling, for the first time in its life it felt good about something, it felt good about hating everything but at the same time resented 'evolving'.

Kate shouted over to Sarah. "Bank to the right Sarah, Rachel and I will draw them off to the left. That'll confuse them hopefully, when we get to the tree's we can re-group and make our next move."

Sarah shouted out to her sister. "Pincer move! That good with you Rach?"

Rachel shouted back excitedly. "Like when we first met?"

Sarah nodded to Rachel. "Yep!" and thought to the Jasban 'Pincer game Jasban.' The Jasban thought nothing else back but a toothy grin spread across his face. Sarah knew in that moment they were set for the next move.

Rachel shouted back. "I'm good, just stay safe!" With that Kate and Conquester peeled off with Rachel to the left, the Jasban continued hurtling towards the forest ahead, as Sarah banked right with the Drask sticking close by.

Kate hollered loudly. "Pincer move now?" The Drask took this moment to stop, they seemed to flatten out disappearing into the foliage of the forest floor.

Rachel responded equally loudly. "Just watch out, with any luck this will be the end of these two Dragons!" Kate knew a pincer move, she was just amazed that these two 'children' knew what that was and wasn't sure that they even knew how to execute one.

The Dragons faltered not knowing in which direction to fly, thankfully for Sarah both followed Kate. Sarah thought down to Brian. 'It's working, 'Pincer time!' Brian knew exactly what Sarah meant and slowed down a little as he changed direction to fall in line behind the Dragons chasing Rachel and Kate. Sarah wasn't about to let anything hurt her little sister, that was for sure! The Drask changed its flow and followed them a tentacles length behind.

Kate and Rachel were nearly at the woods when the first dragon belched out its fire at the fleeing pair and the Jasban could feel the heat on his rump as the Dragon closed in.

Rachel turned and saw the scaly underside of this amazing but terrifying creature swooping up from the first burn only to see the second swooping down for the second and closer burn. The Jasban thought to her. 'I'm going to stop very quickly Rachel so hold on tight, when I've stopped and jump off quick. Okay?'

Rachel gripped hard and thought back. 'Okay but don't get yourself hurt Jasban, not for me or anything right?'

Jasban let out a purr which, although is not an easy thing to do going at that speed, Rachel still felt vibrate through her whole self. As he reached the edge of the wood he thought out, 'Now!' then dug his claws into the grass leaving score marks in the earth behind him as he slid round and came to a very brief halt. After that everything seemed to happen in slow motion for Rachel.

She jumped down from the Jasban just as the fire belching Dragon released its torrent of flame, it overshot them both. Kate was way ahead of the heat as the Jasban sprang up onto a tree trunk and pushed off again into the air to catch the Dragon, sinking his claws deep into its belly.

The surprised creature screeched in pain and began to fall from the air, it seemed unable to co-ordinate its wings. Within seconds its eyes turned from jet black to the normal red and steel blue of most Black Dragons. The Alder had left its mind and it was free, yet the Dragon was now in more peril with the Jasban's weight pulling it down towards the ground. It let out a bloodcurdling scream into the other dragon's mind, that everyone else could hear. 'HELP ME!'

The Jasban knew immediately that the Dragon's mind was free of the Alder and was no longer a threat to Sarah. He retracted his steely claws out of the desperately flapping Dragon's belly and dropped to the ground turning in mid-air as a domestic cat would, landing on all fours surprisingly lightly. He knew the wounds he had inflicted were terrible and probably even fatal.

Kate and Conquester had turned and were galloping back to Rachel as the remaining Alder mind-infested Dragon came around to swoop down again. It spotted the other Dragon struggling to fly, bleeding and falling gently to the ground. He tried to slow himself by flapping his enormous spiked wings backwards in an attempt to protect himself from the advancing Unicorn.

As Rachel watched the scene unfold above, she saw Sarah with her eyes glowing bright blue with intensity as Brian rode up into the air. Brian swung his head, catching the Dragon from behind with his alicorn and ripping through the flesh of the beast's rear left leg.

The Alder immediately left the mind of the Dragon which, unlike its mate fell heavily and painfully to the ground, its wings flapping just twice in the air which was just enough to save it from getting any more hurt. His injury was fearfully painful but not fatal.

Kate and Conquester came to a halt by Rachel just as Sarah and Brian hit the ground cantering around the grounded Dragons. Sarah thought her challenge out so that everyone could hear but addressed the Dragons directly. 'You have a problem with us Dragons? You want to continue this fight now that your minds are free? Come on Reptiles, we are ready for a fight!'

The second wounded Dragon responded into their minds. 'No human, no! We have been used against our will!' It turned and crouched down bleeding from its belly and rolled to its side trying to use its wing to stay upright. 'Leave us alone this is not our fight. This feels like my time to die!'

Kate ran to the beast and shouted for the others to stay clear, she stood in front of the dying dark heavily armoured scaly Dragon and said out loud. "You are right Dragon but we can't right every wrong. We are running out of time so let me try to help you, I don't want you to die."

The Dragon had landed painfully and snorted into her mind. 'What can a puny soft creature like you do for me Human? I am dying, the Jasban has killed me!'

Kate then stroked her hand lightly down the wounds on the belly of the beast, gently running her hands along each of the cuts that the Jasban had inflicted, as she did so the scales of the Dragon welded themselves back together, the bleeding slowed then stopped. Kate then walked to stand in front of the head of the Dragon. 'We never meant you any harm beast, the Alder are our enemy and I have done what I can for you. You will live but you will suffer whilst you heal. Our fight is not with you.'

The Dragon breathed deeply and thought back. 'We, I, will remember this moment human, what you have done for me, though the pain remains.' With no further words she righted herself then flapped her wings to rise with the other Dragon and took to the skies leaving the six companions behind.

Sarah shook her head in confusion and some annoyance, after all Dragons had been the enemy since she was a sproglet! "We have to get to the Ravine, that is our only purpose right now so let's do that shall we?"

She thought down to Brian. 'Can you take us to the Ravine, to my and Jack's home? The Bevy of Dragons will be on our tail soon and we need to have some protection.'

Brian snorted. 'Wherever we are going we have to go there now or hide, look!' All heads turned and looked through the canopy of purple trees to see the horde of Dragons flying towards them, un-mistakable against the backdrop of the two glowing orange suns.

Sarah looked at her friends and then up through the canopy that the Dragons were now burning down with their breath and she spoke out loud to everyone. "Brian, we have no time to find a hiding place, we have to go, now! We have to find Robin! Maybe we can make a plan on the run but we have to go NOW!" Brian hesitated for a moment. Sarah sensed his worry and stroked his neck calmly. "If you ever trusted me Brian then trust me now, we have nowhere to hide from them, we have to find Robin and we have to find the 'Box'. To do that we need to get to the Ravine first, we need to collect weapons."

Brian got the message and lowered his head thinking out. 'You want to go by Jack's place? You want to go home?'

Sarah smiled at the word 'home' she was going home to the cave where she had grown up with Jack as her de facto Dad. 'Yes, but for practical reasons, it's on the way, no time for anything else.' This was not a time for hesitation, this was a time for action, everyone got the same message and the troupe fled the forest with Brian leading them first down into a gully that flowed into a stream that became a river through a Ravine that led down to the Creek. He led them away from the danger of the mind infested Dragons but straight towards the danger of the Alder that lived in the caves below the homes of the Dwarves.

CHAPTER EIGHT

Dargal looked up at Robin "I know where to run to boys but…" here he hesitated and looked a tad angry, "You run faster than I can so grab that Hammer by your right hand for me Robin." Robin looked at the slowly approaching monsters, with their tentacles as long as whips waving slowly around on their backs, then glanced down at the hammer and followed Dargal's instructions picking up the weighty weapon. "Keep backing up boys. Robin, when we reach the second door behind us, open it slowly so as not to draw attention and let us through. When John, Clara you and I are all safely through the door, smash off the door handle with the hammer and follow us through, shutting the door behind you, there is no door handle on the other side of that door so make sure that you can follow us. With that door shut 'they' won't be able to come after us, okay?"

. . .

Both boys nodded and continued walking backward really slowly, maintain the distance between them and the advancing nightmares.

"It's an escape tunnel." The Dwarf continued in a low voice and turned to the Jasban. "Jasban, you will need to run quickly, are you ready?"

The Jasban continued slowly backing up, alert and staying ready to attack if needs be. 'I'm ready little warlord. Will we meet up at the Creek?'

The Dwarf grinned. "If we live through this then we will meet you there." He watched the Alder creeping rapidly towards and around them then as he came level with the second door he shouted out. "Okay run Jasban, the rest of you follow me!"

With that John, Dargal and Clara ran through into the escape tunnel. John held the door "I've got the door Robin." Robin wasted no time but swung the hammer round and down with mighty force onto the handle and smashing it into a pile of broken pieces strewn across the floor.

. . .

John continued, "Come on quick before…" but his words were cut off before Robin could even move an inch as the door slammed shut trapping Robin in the armoury.

Robin looked up to see a huge Alder gripping the ceiling above him its long-clawed hands withdrawing slowly from having shut off Robin's escape route. Robin thought that his heart was going to beat itself out of his chest as the creature turned its huge head down to look at him with its shiny obsidian black eyes that seemed to bore straight through him. It paused and snarled a grin of triumph.

He could hear Clara's panicked voice screaming into his mind. 'Robin boy, Robin!' as her huge fists pounded on the door next to him but it was too late, the Alder flung out a tentacle which cracked like a whip on Robin's shoulder splitting his skin and knocking him backwards. He shouted out in pain but held up his sword with his good arm, it felt like a pointless threat against his vicious enemy.

The other Alder began gathering around, moving closer and closer as the one above him crept down the side of the wall, its long quivering tentacles dislodging weapons from their racks which clanged noisily to the cave floor as it approached.

. . .

Robin let the hammer drop from his hand and quickly grabbed at another huge sword, waving both weapons at the Alder in a gesture of true defiance. He was utterly alone now and there were at least ten of them. One of his attackers crept around to his right side trapping him so that even if he could run faster than a cheetah, he wouldn't be able to escape.

The Alder by the side of him whipped out another tentacle but this time Robin was ready. Through the pain, sweat and panic he felt he swung the sword in his right-hand round with all the strength he could muster and managed a strike that sliced off half of the creature's muscular limb. Robin gained back some of his bravery, paused and then roared his defiance. "Come on creeps, you want to do this? I'll cut every one of you before I die!" He waved both swords in the air but his left arm felt weak as more blood oozed out of the wound and down his arm with every movement he made.

The Alder spoke creepily into his mind. 'We now know that the Slayer is back here in this world and we are going to find, torture and kill her. You, human child, are a treat for us to feast upon, we can easily kill you but why deny us your pain? You are alone and we can feed off of you, just a few more minutes of pain for you, then we will end your misery. If you resist us the pain will go on longer and be much worse!'

Robin looked around the enormous cavern at the creatures slowly stalking towards him, his heart pounded in his chest and then he remembered something stupid. He remembered Rachel's words and John echoing them sarcastically. "Work with what you have Robin, not with what you think you should have!" He took a deep breath and slowed himself. He remembered Sarah and how she had confronted the Dragon in Rachel's shed, how she had pulled a car up a street and how she had ridden a giant White Tiger who she was friends with. "Your Slayer is the girl that I love and with my dying breath I will kill as many of you as I can to help her!" his eyes flamed blue and he called out "Bring it on scumbags!"

One Alder sprang forwards and Robin's arms were a blur as he sliced the head and tentacles from this predator in a swirl of moves. The blood of a Unicorn swirled through his veins as he dispatched another enemy with a sword thrust through its huge black eye and out of the back of its skull. He drew back the sword with a squelching sound and plunged both of his swords into another Alder that screeched in pain as it slumped down surprised by the strength and ferocity of this human boy.

. . .

His bravery was short lived though as another Alder whip cracked another tentacle into the centre of Robin's back ripping through his shirt and leaving a bleeding gash. Robin yelped in pain, another Alder, this one directly in front of him, reared up and spun itself round like a whirlwind, its razor like tentacles swept across Robins face and he fell backwards, three deep cuts in his cheek bled down his face.

Everything hurt but he managed to cut something off another creature, his vision was becoming blurred as blood seeped from his face into his eyes. The Alder moved in, not for the kill but for the pleasure of torture and to feed off Robin's pain.

Robin felt giddy and began to lose consciousness. Seeing this one of the Alder slipped a clawed hand under Robin's chin and slowly lifted his bloodied face up towards its own huge black eyes, Robin had just enough energy left to spit right into the eye of the creature which reeled back for a moment and then swung one of its tentacles round from its back to strike Robin in his ribs, the pain was intense.

Robin fell bleeding and groaning to the hard-stone floor his mind barely functioning now. An Alder moved in to shake

CHAPTER NINE

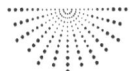

Up from the twisted trees of the lazy forest flew flocks of squawking, silver, shining birds, disturbed by the sound of Sarah approaching with her troupe, they filled the sky.

She led them into a gully that ran from the surface of the world down to the bottom the Creek, this in itself was like a new world. The gully became a ravine as they travelled further down, it had a fast running stream of water that ran through the woods and down to the creek below. The two suns shone through the purple tree branches on either side and reflected off the water. Everything down here seemed brighter and more vibrant somehow.

They came to a wall of hanging Drop weeds that Sarah and Brian headed towards. She turned to her little sister. "This is my home Rach, this is where Jack and I lived for 8 years." Rachel looked around the small valley that they were in. Sarah grabbed at a Drop weed vine and pulled it down which in turn opened a curtain of vines revealing a large cave entrance.

The Jasban under Rachel drooled (as he often did) and thought out. 'Jack is clever, so this is why we could never find you two.' He looked around in awe as they went into 'Sarah's place'.

As Kate's Unicorn walked through the opening she too looked around. "Jack is a resourceful man looking at this place. You must have had a great childhood growing up here!"

It was strange to come from the forest into this well-ordered large room that would not have been out of place in the world they had just come from. There was a table and chairs in the centre of the enormous room and piles of parchments were stacked neatly on shelves around the walls. To one side Jack had redirected water from the stream that ran into a large stone bowl and fell like a small waterfall, running across the cave floor it continued its journey back into the stream outside. Kate and Sarah dismounted, Kate walked the Unicorns to the water trough whilst Sarah went over to Rachel.

One vine that Jack and Sarah had trained to run through the cave had square fruit growing from it and there were rows of mushrooms on either side of the room that grew out from the walls.

There were vine curtains hanging at various places around the walls that hid other rooms, this was a room big enough for all of them, including the Drask, to fit into comfortably.

Rachel looked around. "This place is amazing Sarsy!" She slid off the back of the Jasban who loped over to the vines and expertly knocked two fruit down from them, then sat down on his haunches to eat whilst the Unicorns stood with Kate by the water and drank deeply. The Drask settled down leaning into each other to rest and lowered their heads like they were about to meditate. The Jasban remembered himself and knocking off another couple of fruits, flicked them through air and watched as the Drask caught them without even turning to look.

Sarah walked over to one the curtains and drew it back to slip a hook around to keep it open. "Maybe one day I'll be able to tell you about how Jack taught me to read at that table and about the games we used to play but right now," she paused and looked inside the room, "right now we need weapons. Come here sis."

Rachel walked over to Sarah and looked into the room beyond, it was full of ropes, clamps, swords, hammers, longbows with arrows in bags, poles and two workbenches with an array of homemade tools all left neatly in their well-ordered places. Sarah grabbed a Bow, tested it and then gave it to Rachel. "Here, I made this one when I was thirteen years old so it should be about the right size for you. Grab an arrow and I'll give you a very quick lesson, then we had better grab a few bits to take with us. If we are going to save Robin we will probably have to fight these creatures."

Rachel took the bow from her sister who stood behind her and helped her nock an arrow. "Do you really think he's still alive?" she said as Sarah placed Rachel's fingers on the taught string. "He didn't look too well when we last saw him."

Sarah guided her sisters' arm. "Aim at that board on the other side of the room and see if you can get the arrow to hit the middle of it." Rachel strained pulling back on the string. "He's got to be alive Rachel because I feel something that is more than just 'like' for him." She said this as casually as if she had just said "Let's have some cake."

Rachel half turned in utter shock and let go of the arrow which missed its target, ricocheted off a metal urn and imbedded itself deeply into the surfaced of a work bench. "What! But he's an idiot!"

Sarah deftly picked another arrow from a quiver next to her and placed it in Rachel's hand. "I know Sis but he's kind and funny and ever since I came back to your world, he's the only one apart from you that has made me feel really good. He always makes me smile, when he's around I sort want to hug him. Now, this time keep your aim steady and pretend that you are aiming at something really annoying."

Rachel replaced the arrow, pulled back the string, aimed and steadied herself then let the arrow fly. It flew straight and hit the very centre of the target, Rachel and Sarah stared at the arrow in quite some surprise and Sarah whispered. "Wow Rach, you're a natural. What was the annoying thing that you were thinking of?"

Rachel lowered the bow. "Robin's face!" she said and then smiled at her sister who laughed. "Best we go and find him then, but before we go is there anything to eat around here, I'm starving."

Sarah hugged her sister "I don't know what we're walking into Rach but we've got Kate and good friends and I promise that I won't let anyone kill you." Rachel just hugged her sister back. "Come on" said Sarah pulling Rachel out of the room whilst picking up another bow and a couple of quivers of arrows for them both. "We can grab some fruit on the way out.

CHAPTER TEN

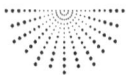

Clara Frab slapped around in panic and frustration and hammered on the door that remained solidly shut. Dargal drew back. "It's no use Clara, these doors are made to resist an attack from everything and anything nasty, we'll never get it open. Robin's on his own."

Clara looked at Dargal and thought out to him with tears in her eyes. 'But Clara Frab must help Robin, Clara Frab promise to stay with Robin' then banged her huge fists against the door loudly. Then they heard it, the roar! It was so loud that it made even the heavily iron clad door shake. All three stood in shock just staring at it for what felt like several minutes but was only seconds, the door shook again but this time it was like something had smashed into it really hard. It sounded like the door had been hit by a huge truck, it buckled in under the impact, but held firm. Everything fell silent.

John stumbled back from the door "What was that Dargal?"

Dargal stared at the door. "I know that roar boy and Robin knows that roar. The creature that just hit the door is immensely strong, a very old friend and a powerful force, if it's who I think it is then Robin may just have a chance, if not, if it was something else that hit this door then...!"

John leaned heavily against the wall looking down at his feet and wondering what to do next, what could they do? He thought about that annoying kid behind the door and how hard he had been trying to save everyone, now he might be dead, or worse just suffering. Every unselfish bone in John's body screamed into his mind and he knew that Robin was a good kid and he, John, needed to do everything he could to save him, if he was still alive and then a thought occurred to him. "Dargal, you said this takes us up to the surface, to the Creek!"

Dargal sat on a step in the corridor that was lit by Dwarvian stones and led up via a stone staircase to the surface. "Yes boy, I did" he took his helmet off and sunk his head into his hands.

John continued. "Is that far from your home and…" he searched his memory of what he had seen in the Alder's mind that had infested his own, "and that's where the Alder are isn't it? Under your cave you said?"

Dargal nodded. "Yes boy but deep under. How does that help us?"

John didn't think to stop himself; he was just connecting

up the dots. "It was you that released the Esmer Alder wasn't it, that's one of the memories of these things, you dug too deep looking for something and found her cave, didn't you? You woke her up, their Guardian!"

Dargal stood up sharply and stared at John in disbelief, he paused and then said. "Yes, but it was an accident." He stared at John for a second or two and then blurted out. "It's all my fault, right from the start, all of it! I dug down further than any Dwarf should and released the ancient Witch, now the boy out there might be dead because of me." He sat down again. "You should kill me now, I brought all of this upon us all and I am so sorry, I have put everyone in danger. Take your sword now and…"

John was only half listening. "No shh! That's not important now, the point is, that is where she was protecting 'The Box', we have to get to that box and open it. I think, Robin said that he had to open 'The Box' and that would kill all of the monsters or something like that." John stood up and began walking around in a circle. "I think that will stop them from mind jumping at least. If we want to help Robin we have to do it quickly, then they will come after us and it may give him a chance to escape. If he is still alive by then!"

Dargal look at Robin in utter disbelief. "We have a chance of saving Robin?"

John started running up the stairs. "Yes, but only if we can get to that box quickly." He thought out to Clara 'Clara will you help?' Clara nodded furiously 'can you bring Dargal he's not as fast a runner as we are' without asking Dargal she scooped him up and swung him round onto her back, as Dargal left the floor he just managed to grab his helmet off the ground.

He clung onto Clara's back and shouted up to John. "Wait boy, we want to go down not up, there's a quicker route to her cave but we have to go down."

John stopped dead in his tracks and bounded back down the stairs two at a time. "How long will it take us to get there?"

Clara turned and started slap slapping down the stairs with Dargal clinging on for dear life. "Minutes but we're going to get wet, can you swim?"

John nodded and all three headed down the staircase the further down they went the wider it became, John began to hear water flowing to the left of them, he started to see water trickling down the rocks, the deeper they went the louder the rush of water became. A minute later they found themselves running next to a fast-flowing underground stream.

As John looked down, he could see that the staircase came to an abrupt halt twenty steps or so ahead, he slowed down only to discover he was standing at the edge of a precipice with the water next to him flowing over the edge, falling down in a waterfall some twenty or thirty feet into a turbulent pool below. He looked confused. "How are we going to get down there?"

Dargal shouted at him from Clara's back. "Jump boy!"

John looked over to Dargal. "Are you nuts! Look how far down that is!" even just looking over the edge made his stomach churn. "I can't jump, I have a fear of heights!" but Dargal had already jumped from Clara's shoulder into the icy waters below.

Clara thought out to John. 'Clara not have scared of heights, John hold breath.' Without stopping she grabbed Johns forearm and pulled him over the edge to the sound of John screaming out in shock and terror. "Clara Noooo! Arrrrgh!"

As they hit the water John's body nearly seized up on him as all of his muscles seemed to contract at once. Dargal was the first to reach the surface and began furiously swimming for the shore. Clara used her huge hands like paddles and quickly broke the surface with John gasping for air a second later, she dragged him through the water and up onto the edge of the pool.

John was breathless but managed to gasp out through chattering teeth to Clara. "You! I didn't, that was, oh my…" but gave up trying to speak as the shivering took hold of him and his teeth began to chatter quite loudly. Clara wrapped herself around John, hugging heat back into his body from her own whilst Dargal shook himself dry in a series of odd vibrations, just like a dog exiting a pond.

Clara's back seemed to glow red and John felt a warmth begin to spread through him. After a few minutes he was beginning to warm up and calm down. Clara unfurled herself from him and smiled 'Clara help John yes?'

John didn't quite know what to say to this innocent creature that had just nearly killed him, but he smiled knowing that he was still alive and thought out to her. 'Yes, Clara helped John'.

After a few minutes of calming down and warming up Clara stood and pulled John to his feet 'Good, now we help Robin, yes!'

John looked at up the waterfall he had just survived. "Dargal I hope that you have another way back, because that looks like a one-way journey to me."

"There is another way boy." Dargal bridled angrily "The tunnel that I dug to get down here, that has caused all of this trouble! I should have stopped when we had enough space for all of the Dwarves to live in, I should have been content, but no, I had to go on digging didn't I, I had to…"

John cut him off. "Robin once said to me 'Work with what you have and not with what you think you should have' so how about you forgive yourself and we can all work together to put this right, okay?"

Dargal stared up at the boy for a moment as he felt forgiven, somehow, for the sins in his mind. "Now I have a Human boy teaching me what I should already know!" He walked up to Robin and put his hand out. "I would like to call you friend boy."

John looked down at this impossible Dwarf and smiled, he felt like he had just been accepted by someone incredibly important and if he had an inkling of Dargal's history he would have realised that he was right.

He took the Dwarves small hand and shook it and got much more than an inkling. "Thank you Dargal, you really are a remarkable person to know, I feel honoured." A tingle travelled up his arm and then he dropped to his knees in a mental body shock as a montage of Dargal's memories flooded into his mind. It was like having an entire life history embed itself into his brain, his eyes widened as Dargal's memories became a part of his own.

Dargal grinned. "We Dwarves like to share our lives wisdoms. It helps the people we share with improve theirs."

John beamed a smile at Dargal and Dargal smiled straight back. It took John several moments to come back to his senses. "Thank you Dargal, that, I.." he looked down trying to find the right words "It's just such an honour!" Then took a deep breath and calmed himself. "Okay now how do we get to the witches cave?"

Dargal smiled grimly at John. "Look up boy, we are already here!"

John looked up to see what looked like hundreds of pairs of bright white eyes staring down at him from the roof of the vast cavern they were now in. He held his breath and just stared up at the eyes.

The Alder had their elongated claw like hands sunk into the roof of the cave and just hung like bats with the tentacles on their back slowly swaying back and forth in the air. John started to walk slowly backwards. "Dargal" he whispered "We've got to get out of here!"

Dargal was squeezing water out of his shirt and flapping it dry. "Don't worry John. They can't see or hear us. Only when their big old eyes turn black do we need to worry, that's when they are awake."

John kept staring up at the roof of the cave. "But there are so many of them, I didn't realise. I knew that they think like a hive but I didn't know…"

Dargal put his shirt back on and slipped back into his armour as easily as putting on a coat "So this box boy, where is it?"

John had to tear his eyes away from above him. "It's whatever it was that she, it, was resting on, that's why she was resting on it, to protect it."

Dargal thought for a moment. "That thing! I know where that is, come with me, that thing is in the cave that leads up to my home, though how you would open something like that 'Box' I don't know?"

Dargal headed of into a side cave with John and Clara following close behind. In it they saw the 'Box' just sitting opposite the tunnel that Dargal had made so long ago. "You mean this?" he pointed to a huge stone oblong that was nearly as tall as John and at least ten feet long.

John looked at it. "It looked smaller in the memory of the Alder, I guess because they are so large." Walking around it, it seemed to be just a solid block of rock. He tentatively reached out and touched it but it wasn't actually just solid. Where he touched a pile of dust fell off and onto the floor revealing an indentation. He looked at Dargal then at Clara and then back at Dargal. "It's covered in thick dust, quickly help me brush it down."

Dargal wasted no time and set about rubbing his hands over the stone and as the dust fell it covered the small Dwarf (he sneezed wildly). A set of symbols were revealed on the side of the 'Box' that no-one understood. Symbols that were of no language that they knew or even anything like they had ever seen before. Robin brushed the dust from the top and then stood back to study them. "Any idea's Dargal?"

Dargal stood next to Robin. "Well not really, they look more like pictures than words though."

Robin nodded but said nothing for a few moments then thought out to Clara. 'Any idea's what these symbols might mean Clara?'

Clara smiled and thought back. 'Only one symbol.' and she pointed to the fourth symbol. 'That one Frab.'

John looked more closely and sure enough it did sort of resemble a curled up Frab. He looked at the other symbols. One looked like a fallen tree with a straight line above it another looked like a wiggly line with a pile underneath it and the last one was even more baffling and was at the centre of the other symbols, it was two wiggly lines with a 'V' between them.

Dargal looked at Clara and John and said. "Well boy, can you open this thing? We have to hurry because God knows what those vile creatures are doing to Robin. I have to tell you though that the witch was pure evil, she would make us torture ourselves so that she could feed from our pain, so if these things have Robin I fear for his very sanity!"

John frowned deeply. "I don't know, I don't know?" Then

he looked at Clara and then back at the other symbols and he walked away and then back again looking at the different pictures and then it hit him like a bolt of lightning and his brain fizzed a bit in pleasure of understanding a stupidly easy puzzle that was as stupidly difficult to understand. "It's the elements! Earth, Clara the rock, wind, a fallen tree, fire a burnt down tree and the last is water, a creature drowning in a river, that last line is pointing up but not like an arrow, it's just a line and it's pointing up to?" he ran his hands up the side of the box to a small well in the top of the rock, then he noticed that the well had a tiny hole in it.

Dargal looked sceptical. "That's what you see is it, from those scratchings, if you are right then you are a genius?!"

John ignored him and thought out to Clara. 'Can you bring some water from the pool Clara? As much as you can carry in your hands!'

Clara wasted no time and slap slapped her way back to the pool, scooped up what she could in her hands and then did a thing no Frab had ever done before and which looked like a very difficult manoeuvre, she 'walked upright' all be it with trepidation, back to John using only her two lower legs. When she eventually reached John, she looked at him and asked. 'What now John boy?'

John grinned. 'When I say. 'Now' drop the water on to the top of this rock then make sure you have Dargal nearby because we may have to run really, really fast ok?' Then he spoke to Dargal "I'm not sure if this will work but if it does then that box will open and it will stop acting as a beacon for the Alder. Whatever is in this thing will escape and they won't be able to mind jump anymore. Do you understand what I mean Dargal?"

Dargal looked at John for several moments until the horror of what John was saying sunk into the small Dwarf's brain. "They'll wake up, all of them..." He looked back at the cave that was full of the huge bat like monsters and then back at John, "...and they will come for us!"

John nodded. "Yes, they will, can we out run them or hide or something? I need to know now Dargal because the ones that have Robin, will also know we have opened the 'Box'. This is the distraction we needed but they too will come for us, if they still live, so my friend, will we be able to escape the swarm when they come? Robin said to 'Open the box, kill all the monsters' so maybe just opening the box will kill them all but if it doesn't, can we outrun them?"

Dargal stared at John and then looked down at the ground and started walking around the rock talking to himself. "No, we can't outrun them, there are thousands of them, all bigger than humans and nastier than a squashed Cratalorg. Hmm!"

Then a familiar voice came into all of their minds as the Jasban loped into the cave. 'I've been looking for you lot, where's Robin?'

John ran to the Jasban grabbing and hugging him around the neck and thought out to him. 'We are so pleased to see you Jasban! Robin is in trouble and the only way we can help him is to open this box, which I think we can do but if we do manage to do it then the swarm of Alder will be on us in seconds and none us will survive!'

Dargal thought out to the Jasban, John and Clara. 'We need to run then, the moment you open that box, if you can, then they'll know and they'll come for us, I know you are fast Jasban but do you think you can outrun them carrying the three of us?'

The Jasban looked at them all and then loped into the larger cave to look up at the sleeping Alder, he turned back to the others and thought back. 'Chase game, you kidding? Bring it on!'

John nodded at Clara who poured her huge handfuls of water onto the box and as she did so it crackled and creaked and then nothing happened. They all stood and waited expectantly for a few moments, nothing. 'More water Clara, we need more water'

Clara slap slapped her way back to the pool and scooped up more water but as she did so she looked up and saw several white eyes blinking out to a dark blackness, the Alder were waking up and then she performed that amazing manoeuvre of walking on two legs again, slowly back moving back to the oblong rock. She thought out to everyone. 'Monsters waking up, run soon yes?'

Robin nodded as his heart beat faster and thought back. 'Yes Clara, we run very soon, drop the water onto the stone.' Clara put her hands over the centre of the stone and let the water flow into the little well. It seeped into every crevice and covered every symbol. Nothing happened for a few moments and then a light began to glow from the edges of the rock, it got brighter and brighter as seconds passed. The most amazing warbling sound came from the box like the warmest call of the smallest bird and the sound grew.

Then the first Alder appeared at the entrance to the cave that held the box then began moving menacingly forwards towards them as the troupe moved slowly backwards away from it.

The Jasban moved in front of everyone protectively. A rasping voice spoke into their minds. 'You humans are stupid to come here. Now you will suffer.'

Dargal spat back. "I'm no human, monster and we're not ready to die!' He drew he small sword out and lifted it towards the Alder that towered above them. Its tentacles waving around in the air dangerously close to them.

John looked at Dargal and then back at this huge creature, its black eyes boring into him. "But we are not 'The Slayer' you want the 'Slayer' don't you?"

The Alder hissed. 'We can smell the Slayer, she is here in this world again and she will also suffer and die then one of us will rise to become the new Queen, the new Esmer!' It moved sideways as if to get around the Jasban. The Jasban turned to block access to his friends and snarled with teeth bared.

Another Alder dropped down to the entrance then another. They started moving forwards crawling into the cave, then came to a sudden halt when from nowhere a dark shadow fell over and around them. They seemed surprised and John could feel a palpable rage rising like the Darkness, the shadow was somehow alive.

It seemed to hover above the Alder causing them to wait as it dropped then writhed around them and as it did so two of them imploded violently! The troupe watched in amazement and stepped back, John touched the lid of the Box as more Alder dropped from the ceiling of the huge cave next door and were slowly engulfed by the darkness.

Their attention was dragged away from the unexpected help to the sound of grinding stone and they all looked to see Clara pushing as hard as she could against the lid of the box. It moved. She shouted out. 'Rock not rock, rock trap!' As it moved the light from inside grew brighter and John could feel anger in the Darkness grow and turned to help Clara.

Both of them pushed as hard as they could as slowly the lid of the box slid away and crashed to the floor, as it did the whole room was filled with an eye piercing light, within the light that rose from the box the shape of a creature emerged.

The Darkness suddenly turned its attention from the invading Alder and swept itself down to writhe in front of John and Clara and in their minds many thousands of years of pain found its relief and its voice filled their minds in a thank you that was filled with sorrow and rage.

The Darkness then rose up to the join with the light. The sight was beautiful to behold as the two creatures melded together in a swirl of love becoming one, everyone in the cave felt a strange relief almost on behalf of the two creatures that were now 'one' being.

John looked over to Dargal with wide eyes. "That is not what I expected to happen but Wow!"

Dargal just stared at the creature "It is an 'Elemental' I am sure. The Alder must have somehow split it in two millennia ago!"

Then a voice that was more of a feeling than a language entered their minds and they felt the creature feel its freedom, it floated through the air in the cave as if it was just enjoying the space to move and it emanated pure joy. It was huge and as it passed them it stopped briefly in front of Clara then swirled around her and John. Clara put her huge wet hands out to touch the light and John could see that her feet were no longer on the ground and nor were his, she was beaming out a smile to it and thought out so everyone could hear. 'Creature free now, Alder not trap creature anymore, creature free now!'

John turned from this amazing sight to the entrance through which they had come in, Alder were gathering but none of them dare enter their cave. Clara and John's feet touched the ground at the same time and she thought out again this time directly to Dargal. 'Alder use creature to mind jump for long time but no more, creature free at last!'

The creature seemed to notice the gathering Alder for the first time and the light strobed red and black displaying its anger to all present. It left Clara and John, flying directly at its captors who briefly tried to flee but the light was way too quick, it seemed to envelope one Alder after another but only for a second, as one by one the Alder exploded and the light swirled onto its next victim. The remaining Alder started to flee the area as quickly as they could, they crawled across the cave walls and ceiling to escape certain death.

After the carnage the light flowed back to the 'Box' that had held it captive for so very, very long and struck it with a force so immense that the box was sent hurtling against the cave wall smashing into pieces. Silence fell on the room.

The creature returned to its former, calmer soft white light and swirled once more around the three of them. This time it revealed its soft and amazing face, smiling with ancient gratitude for what they had done. The face was utterly awe inspiringly beautiful. John held his breath out of pure amazement. The Elemental swirled away, slowly disappearing through the tunnel that led to Dargal's home, out to the surface of the world and freedom from this prison where it had been held for many thousands of years.

John dropped to his knees "Wow! That was awesome, truly awesome!"

Dargal looked around. "That it was John but I don't think the Alder are going to be too happy with us now. They'll be back and soon so we had better get out of here. Quickly everyone let's go."

John stood slowly, still feeling the intensity of the moment. "How can we get back to the Armoury? We have got to find Robin."

Clara slapped around in a circle and thought out. 'Oh no! Clara forget Robin, must help Robin!'

Dargal looked at the tunnel that the light had escaped

through and then crept back to the 'nest' of the Alder. "Same way as that creature, through the tunnel that leads to my old home, then there are several tunnels that lead from the surface back down to the Armoury. We might have a problem when we get up there though!"

John looked back at Dargal. "You have got to be kidding me! What now?"

Dargal looked at the Alder who were all crawling across the floor, walls and ceiling of the vast cave and out into the multitude of tunnels beyond. "I think that the Alder are 'swarming' look at them they're after something, it's like they have the scent of their prey and it's not us."

Before anyone could say anything more Clara thought out. 'Robin more important, now save Robin', then went to scoop Dargal up onto her shoulders ready to flee up through the tunnel.

John shouted out loud. "No wait, Clara, the Alder said that they were intent on killing the Slayer so maybe we need to find her? Maybe we need to find this 'Sarah' now, maybe she's the one that needs our help?"

John paused and looked at Dargal who shrugged and said. "If Sarah is back in this world then she can probably take care of herself. She is an unusual and exceptional human child."

John frowned "Yes, I am getting that impression but if Robin is already dead then…" He didn't get to finish that sentence but found himself on the floor with Clara pinning him down and her rock like fist raised above his head and her other huge hand pressing down on his chest.

Clara spoke slowly into his mind. 'Robin not dead, Robin need Clara, John understand?'

John looked up at her and knew that she could and would snuff him out in a second, and in that very moment he finally realised how utterly devoted to Robin she was and how entirely alien she was. He looked into her Kaleidoscopic eyes and spoke back as gently as he could into her mind. 'I hope so Clara, I really do. You are amazing for being so devoted to him, but we can't fight these monsters alone, we need help and maybe Sarah can help us. Then we can go and find Robin, okay?'

Clara stared into John's eyes for a decisive moment and came to a decision. 'Sarah help find Robin. We find Sarah now.' She still looked down at John on the ground with her fist clenched above him. 'How we find Sarah?'

John didn't take his eyes from hers but said out loud. "Dargal, if Sarah is back where would she go? Please answer quickly because I really need some hope right now!"

Dargal kept a cautious eye on the entrance to the Alder's cave. "The only place Sarah would come to if she came back would be her safe place in the Ravine, to her and Jack's home."

Clara looked at Dargal and thought out. 'Dargal know way?'

Dargal looked back at her. "Yes" he said out loud "It's…"

Clara wasn't waiting and leapt at Dargal lifting him up and headed out of the cave in one surprisingly swift move.

John climbed painfully up onto the back of the Jasban. "Blimey but that rock can shift when she wants to!" He stretched and bent forwards "Ow, every part of me hurts."

The Jasban thought up. 'You want to stop and rest little John?"

John had a bizarre moment of laughter. He was taller than most other teenagers but to the Jasban he was a 'little' creature. "I don't think I dare Jasban. I don't want to upset Clara again! Come on let's go." The Jasban didn't waste a second, leaping after Clara, heading to the surface at the bottom of the canyon like creek.

CHAPTER ELEVEN

As Robin fell another Alder struck out with its whip of a tentacle, slicing down the side of Robin's leg. He jerked sharply from the pain of it. His vision was becoming more blurred, the pain in his body dominated his senses. He was starting to lose hope until a thunderous shock of sound filled his entire self with its roar of anger.

He tried to raise himself up and wipe his eyes but the pain was too much and he slumped back down. The Minotaur raged around the Dwarf Armoury, grabbing at the Alder, crushing them to death swiftly then tearing them apart with his bare hands, their vicious tentacles having little effect upon his leathery skin.

. . .

He didn't see the dishevelled Government agent putting down the small form of a Sprite then picking up a sword from a fallen rack. The hefty sword swung around in a whirling dervish of expertly trained accuracy, striking the Alder and sending them to their death.

He didn't see 'The horned beast' grabbing a tentacled monster from the ceiling then pinning it to the door and punching his fist through the creature's skull nor did he see the resulting dent in the iron clad door. The last thing he heard was the resounding boom of skull hitting iron, then another and then everything faded into darkness as he lost consciousness.

The Minotaur turned down to Robin, lifting his limp, bleeding body from the cold stones. He woke again briefly and said in a weak whisper. "They want to kill Sarah, Minotaur, they want to kill her!" His words were quite in the noise that was the adrenalin fuelled rage of the Minotaur. The Minotaur leant in further and heard his words. "I failed her Minotaur, I failed Sarah and you and everyone, I'm sorry." Then Robin fell back into blissful unconsciousness.

The Minotaur roared again out of anger and stomped out of the Dwarvian Armoury with Robin in his arms heading for the surface. He wanted revenge and shouted back in the direction of the the Agent. "These monsters need to be crushed and killed!"

The Agent picked up the Sprite that he had carefully laid down hoping that the tiny thing still lived and followed on. He stopped himself for a very brief moment and frowned because this was new. He 'felt' hope….

CHAPTER TWELVE

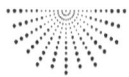

Sarah, Rachel and their friends travelled down a pass that led from the warm surface of the planet, it was known by the locals as Sarah and Jack's Ravine. The pass was a good mile long and steep in places, on either side blue rocky walls rose up with unusual trees and plants of pink and purple foliage growing out of every crevice. The tree canopy ensured that they remained largely hidden from the skies above them. As they descended the path widened out. The trickling steam that ran through the centre, had become a torrential river of turbulent waters by the time it joined the creek itself.

The creek they called it! A fissure in the crust of this planet that encircled it and contained a river without end. The creek held every life form imaginable, as well as some that weren't.

It was an eco-system all of its own and vastly different

from that of the surface of the planet, a world under the world, spreading the width of an 'Earth city' in places. The 'sky' from down here glowed purple and green with cloud formations made up of swarms of insect.

Rachel looked over at Sarah and the reality of their situation started to dawn on her. There was Sarah riding a Unicorn and Kate next to her doing the same whilst she herself rode a terrifying looking vegetarian. They were all headed into trouble, trouble that might see them not come out alive, all in order to save Robin and some other kid they hadn't even met yet.

If the kids at school could see what she was seeing there would not be a mobile phone or a twitter account that wasn't buzzing with total amazement and she knew that there would be a flurry of praise and criticism in equal measure. That's just how this social media stuff worked.

She looked out further down the Ravine and noticed that there was an oddly square patch of Electric Daisies that were crackling in full bloom and said down to the Jasban. "Those Daisies look bright; I wouldn't like to fall into a patch like that!"

The Jasban looked down the Ravine and thought back. 'I think a patch like that might have blown my brother away for good?'

She looked down at the Jasban and thought a private thought out to him. 'You haven't seen your brother for a while Jasban, do you miss him?'

The Jasban stopped dead in his tracks whilst the others

walked on. 'That's an odd question Rachel the Intrepid. Of course I miss him, he is the other half of me, I have all of you, my friends yes, but he is my fun and my Joy. I only live to be reunited with him so that we can play again. So that we can once again be one.'

Rachel looked ahead at Sarah riding Brian like she had ridden a Unicorn every day of her life and thought down to the Jasban. 'I love my sister Jasban but I'm not sure that is enough for her to want to stay with me in the same way. I think I may lose her to your world, to her home and I really don't want that to happen, I want her to always be around to play with me.'

They passed a huge burned out tree and a seriously large boulder that sat precariously balanced in the centre of the stream, it would roll unstoppably down the Ravine were it not for a tiny amount of pebbles holding it in place. Rachel realised in that moment what a dangerous place this could be.

The Jasban sat down abruptly and simply thought. 'Then tell her that now, I tell my brother everything or I would if he were not lost to me now!' Immediately he though out to Sarah. 'Stop now Sarah the Adventurer, your little sister Rachel the Intrepid needs to ask you something.'

Rachel was briefly mortified. 'No.' She thought to the Jasban, 'No, we humans don't do it that way we…'

The Jasban cut off her thoughts with. 'Why not? Just ask her the question and she'll give you the answer.'

Rachel was suddenly experiencing unexpected turmoil and panic. 'But I might not like the answer Jasban.'

Brian and Sarah stopped, Sarah turned in confusion to her sister. 'What is it Sis?'

Rachel slapped the Jasban on the shoulder. 'And I didn't mean now!' Then looked over to Sarah. "I just need to say…" she faltered for a moment trying to find the right words, "If we get through this, if we survive this whatever this is, will you be coming home? I mean to our home with Mum and Dad?"

Sarah asked Brian to turn around and faced Rachel full on. "I don't know Rach. That's the long and the short of it, I don't know yet. I want to stay with you always and forever because you are my little sister. I love you and have loved you since before all this began, but I am torn because this is the place that I understand most. Please don't ask me to answer that question now because I don't know but know that I do love you Rachel the Intrepid and I always will."

Rachel stared at her sister in dismay, then looked up out of sheer frustration. She could now see past the thinning canopy of purple trees and her attention, her focus changed. A well organised Bevvy of hundreds of Dragons were beginning their descent towards them, spewing out a wall of fire, the sky was filled with the black mass with even more following on in a seemingly endless flow. Rachel shouted out loud to everyone. "Look up!"

The first Dragon was already nearly upon the troupe, burning down the trees around them whilst several others were following and burning out any remains. These Alder mind infected Dragons were huge and precise in their execution, destroying everything in their path to find Sarah and her companions, but mainly Sarah.

Everyone heard the Alder scream from the minds of the Dragons. 'We can smell you Slayer, we are coming to torture and kill you!'

The group started to run as fast as they could, trying to escape the nightmare above them.

The rasping communal voice of the Alder shouted into their minds from the Dragons above 'You cannot hide from us Slayer, now you will die and whichever one of us kills you will become the new Guardian. We shall kill you slowly whilst we feed on your pain!'

Everyone could feel the cruel joy in that voice in their heads of a collective creature that believed that it had its prey cornered and ready to be tortured and killed.

Sarah sat defiant on Brian's back and shouted out into the mind of the Alder. 'You haven't killed me yet lowlifes and I'm not ready to die!'

The fire from these immense beasts not only burned the tree tops above them but also those before them, the two Unicorns and the Jasban found themselves running simultaneously away from and towards an inferno, the heat was rapidly becoming intense and unbearable.

Kate thought out to everyone. 'Stop! Hold your ground.' As everyone skidded to a halt, she turned on the back of Conquistador, then making a fist threw her arm out in a circle from which a powerful wind swept upwards extinguishing the burning canopy behind them and then repeated the same move aiming this time for the trees in front of them.

The Dragons flew straight over in surprise, then started wheeling around to come back at them, belching out fire as they came. "Any idea's Sarah? I don't know how long I can keep them off us, but it won't be for long!"

Sarah looked up at the impossible scene above them. "The cave in this Ravine is about a minute's ride from here, can you keep them off us for that long? There is an overhang on the cliff face that we can defend ourselves from there."

The rasping voice shouted into their heads once more. 'Don't run Slayer, don't hide, just accept that we have you and you will…' The voice stopped abruptly. They could feel a change in the threat above, it was as if the Alder had just stopped or were gone as a sonic boom rolled out through the world. Everyone not only heard it but could feel it like an earthquake passing through their bodies.

The formations of the Dragons broke apart as if being awakened and released for the first time then the throng turned to fight each other, as normal Dragons do, brutally and fatally. A bloodied and broken Dragon hurtled down from the skies above, its body smashed through the trees that had hidden them so effectively, its scaled mass of breaking bones crashed into Kate and Conquester with an intense force, tumbling them both down the ravine towards the Creek. Everyone could hear as Kate's mind screamed out in panic. 'Conquester, no!'

The blood from the now dead Dragon splattered outwards

even covering Rachel as it spun past and hurtled onwards down through the ravine.

Rachel looked at Sarah stunned and soaked in the Dragons blood and then up to see that the Dragons above were at war with each other. Fire reigned and talons scored as the beasts fought each other for supremacy and power in the air. There was no unity to them anymore, they were fighting amongst each other, as they usually did. Chaos ruled once again in the Dragons!

The girls looked at each other in confusion at what was happening. Kate thought out loud from below them. "The Box, someone has managed to open the Box. The Alder are gone from the Dragons, they are fighting each other but Conquester, oh my God, Conquester!"

Sarah looked bewildered as Rachel shouted out. "Kate! Where are you?"

Both Rachel and Sarah wasted no time as they turned and ran to find their friend. The Drask though fell still and closed themselves into each other, almost like they had just shut down and were absolutely motionless against the storm of fighting Dragons above them.

Rachel and the Jasban were the first to reach Kate and her crushed companion, she jumped down to see Kate bending over the Unicorn that lay next to her, still alive just and struggling weakly to get up.

Rachel was in floods of tears as she went to help the Unicorn. She tried to push Conquester upright but it's hooves just couldn't gain purchase in the soft peaty ground. With every exhausting attempt it slid back down, she shouted at Kate. "Don't just stand there help me!"

Kate shook her head. "I'm so sorry Rachel but there is nothing I can do, our friend here has more injuries on the inside and I have lost the magic, it was ripped out of me when the Box was opened!"

Rachel shouted back as she continued to push against Conquester the Unicorn. "That can't be true! Help me please, please!"

Kate put her hand upon the forehead of the beautiful white furred beast, spread her fingers out and closed her eyes to concentrate. "I'm so sorry Rachel but it's true. Someone has freed the creature that was in the box and the Alder can't mind jump. There is no magic in me anymore but the creature is free."

Rachel was confused. "What creature, what box? Conquester needs our help, now!"

By the time Sarah and Brian had reached them the Unicorn had stopped trying to struggle to its feet, laying on the ground exhausted and panting.

Sarah slid off of Brian and went to her sister, kneeling down beside her she slid her arm around Rachel's shoulder with her own eyes watering. She took a deep breath and said. "I'm sorry sis, we have to let him go. This is a harsh place to be, Jack and I have had to say goodbye to many creatures here, human and non-human. I am so sorry Rachel."

Kate thought out to them all. 'The magic is gone from me, I can't help, I am so sorry.'

Brian circled at a trot as his friends breathing slowed then he knelt down next to Conquester, bowed his head and passed a private thought into his dying friend's mind, wrapping all of the comfort and love that he could give into that thought which said, 'Goodbye friend.' A thought filled with memories of a thousand years of fun, Unicorn smiles and tears.

Brian then thought out to Sarah, Rachel and Kate. 'Whatever happens above us now with the Dragons will happen, but you three must see this so come and kneel close to me, you need to rest and understand.'

Both girls felt utterly traumatised by everything that was going on. The Dragons continued their battles above, fire and smoke surrounded them as Brian's voice drew them to him. The group sat by the head of the dying Unicorn amongst the scorched and smouldering trees.

Brian continued to speak kindly into their minds. 'My friend is dying and his body will die but we Unicorns do not die like you mortals. Please watch me and then look into my best friends' eye and see what you can see.'

Brian closed his eyes and then seemed to walk out of his own body, the apparition getting smaller the closer that he came to his friend and eventually disappearing into his friends' eye.

All three looked into the eye of the dying unicorn and were stunned by what they saw. The world of fire and fury surrounding them seemed to melt away and they saw deep in his eyes a scene that would never leave them, a scene where

Brian and Conquester galloped along an expanse of deeply green and luscious grass, then up into and down out of the air, slowing they gradually came to a halt.

As they did so they raised their heads and gently nestled into each other's manes for a moment. Then moving away from each other they bowed. As the humans watched the picture in the eye of the dying unicorn they saw its spirit leaving his own physically crushed body with Brian's and then both spirits cantered into a herd of other ghostly Unicorns that seemed to have been waiting to receive Conquester. The herd moved as one, cantering back up their ravine, the image of Brian turned around whinnied his final goodbye to the herd and ran back towards them. His image emerged from the now still form of his friend and re-joined his own body, he breathed a blue breath as his eyes reopened. Conquester's eyes closed peacefully for the final time.

As Rachel smoothed her hands gently over the body of the dead Unicorn she found herself looking up at the boy with amazingly blue eyes. Brian looked her deeply in the eye and said to her mind. 'We are Unicorn' Rachel the Intrepid, we do not die, we just move on so do not be so sad.' The boy faded from her mind back into the form of her friend Brian.

Rachel did cry though, she cried for the Unicorn, she cried for her sister, for herself not having her Mum and Dad there and everything being so crazy. Sarah hugged her little sister as Kate looked on and understood. Rachel was young and no 14-year-old should have to bear this burden, no matter how amazing they were. For a few short moments the group said and did nothing.

Kate took a deep levelling breath, leaned down and hugged her dead soul mate then pulled herself together, putting the grief she felt to one side, she thought out to the group. 'The Dragons are no longer a threat but if the Alder can't mind jump and use other creatures as their weapons then they will swarm like bees to find Sarah. Until you are dead, they can't make a new queen or guardian. To find your friend Robin we might have to face that swarm and if we do, we will need an army of friends. I know what they are, these Alder, they are utterly evil and we few can't defeat them. Of that I am pretty sure.

Sarah squeezed her sister in a big hug, then stood up, looked at the chaos of Dragons above and then down to the creek where the real Alder would no doubt be coming from soon. "We have friends Kate. Whether they will help us, or even know that we are here I don't know but from the Bobadon to the Frow we have friends here."

Turning around Sarah grabbed her sisters' arm and pulled her to her feet. "Little sister of mine, Rachel the Intrepid, I believe in you and how clever you are." Then she turned to look at Kate. "You are strange to me Kate, but I trust you and you must trust me now because I know this world. Will you do that Kate even without your magic, we still have our friendship and that counts more than magic, will you do that?" Kate simply nodded.

Sarah continued. "Then I think that we can find Robin

and whoever the kid is. We can turn back this swarm of nasties because, well, there's nothing else we can do. We have got to get on and do what we can, we have to work with what we have got and not with what we think we should have. You two, Brian, the Jasban, the Drask and me are all we have right now. I have a few surprises up my sleeve for them, this my home, so let's go with that and see what happens".

She took a deep breath and looked around at the gathering. "None of you are allowed to die protecting me because if I die, they still won't stop, I know that now, I know that this is not all my fault. We are the only creatures in the universe that can stop these Alder, right here and now there is no-one but us to save all of our worlds from becoming the slaves of these things. I think we have no choice but to fight to the death and I believe with all my heart that we can win. Are you with me, will you fight with me to the end my friends?"

Kate smiled. "If you had ever read Shakespeare young Sarah then you would know that was the best ever rallying cry, I'm with you child, let's go face the swarm together." Kate turned to Rachel. "You could go back to Sarah's place, you would be safe there."

Rachel looked out at everyone, at Brian so stoic and magnificent a beast, at the Jasban who she knew would rather die than see her hurt, at the Drask who had brought Kate back to life and were still sitting motionless some way off and at her sister who she had loved from before she knew that she even had a sister. She looked down for a moment then thought out to them all. 'I know that you all think that I am just a child, you are right I am young and every one of you have saved me in one way or another in the past. You all know me in your own ways and you know that I can fight in my own way.'

Then she came to a decision, stood up and looked at each of her friends. "I know Robin is an idiot but he is our idiot and I think we owe it to Mary and Jack to try to find him just as he would try to find anyone of us, wouldn't he, if we were in trouble. He saved me from myself before when he didn't have to, he saved me from her, the witch and he did that because he is an idiot, he is my idiot friend."

Kate and Sarah looked at each other and smiled "Okay Sis, well said and yes I think he would too. Let's go find our idiot and hope that we can find some friends on the way eh?" Without another word everyone started down to the Creek to face whatever came at them and to find their friend and idiot, Robin. Sarah stopped and said back to the Drask who followed them from a distance. "We have asked so much of you Drask but this is not your fight. We would love to see you again if we live but please don't follow us now. We love you and would not like to see you hurt."

The Drask smiled and their huge eyes gleamed as they bowed, lifted a tentacle that reached out and stroked Kate's face. For the first time ever the Drask spoke but not in words, everyone and everything heard the words that were not words but a feeling and it simply said, 'Special like Sarah.' The

Drask lowered it tentacle, drifted back up the Ravine and out of sight.

Kate looked at everyone and smiled. "I have no idea what happened there. Shall we just move on and try to find the boys?" everyone nodded and after a pause looking at Kate with curiosity the group started moving off down the ravine once more to find the boys.

The troupe didn't have to go far though. A boy's panicky voice shouted out and up to them through the crevice from the Creek below as he ran towards them. "Hey there, Hello! Are you Sarah the Adventurer? Because if you are me and Dargal here really need your help!" He looked at Dargal. "Well a Kid called Robin is the one that needs help really and there's a storm of monsters coming for you, we've all got to get out here quick!"

Sarah smiled at Rachel "Dargal's here? Oh Rach, you're going to love Dargal!" Then she looked more closely at the boy and her eyes narrowed as she drew her bow round, selected an arrow nocked it then took aim.

John saw what she was doing from way down the Ravine. Slowing his pace from panicky run to a worried walk he asked Dargal. "What's she doing?"

Rachel looked at Sarah and asked. "What are you doing Sarsy?"

Dargal looked up at John as they both stopped walking, he looked at John with pity. "She's taking aim boy and she never misses; Sarah the Adventure never misses her mark. It's been nice knowing you son, not sure what you have done to upset her but she never misses her mark, see you in the afterlife maybe!" Dargal took one step to the left, looked at Sarah with her bow, looked John up and down, then took another step to the left and said. "Try to fall that way, will you?"

Sarah drew back the bow and eyed her target saying almost absentmindedly. "The last time we saw this boy he had his arm around Robin's neck and was strangling him, wasn't he?"

Rachel looked horrified as the idea of what her sister might be doing dawned on her. "But Sarah you can't...!"

John looked down at Dargal in a sudden panic "But why? What have I..." His words were cut off by Sarah's own shouted thought in his head. 'DUCK!'

Then she let loose her arrow, it flew directly at John's head. Watching her do this with a look of increasing horror on his face he threw himself to the ground and thought. 'What is going on and why does everything want to kill me?'

CHAPTER THIRTEEN

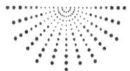

The last Bobadon strode majestically through the creek following its herd, raising and lowering its whale sized head to suck in the airborne sea of insects. It swallowed with an enormous gulp and then slowly lowered its enormous head below the buzzing food mass to take a long slow breath. As it looked down at the ground below, at the now turbulent water that it strode through, he noticed a strange smell. It was as if something old and musty had been released from having been trapped underground for a long, long time. He moved gracefully and slowly onwards to join the rest of the herd, not realising the significance of the smell and the mayhem that was about to take place below.

. . .

The Alder were angry, furious in fact. They were seeking revenge with the fury focused on just one being. Anything and anyone that got in their way as they swarmed out of their ancient hiding places in their hundreds, would suffer until they found 'The Slayer', the one that had killed their Queen.

There was also a new anger on top of that insult that they felt and it was intensifying their rage. Some Human had released the 'Elemental of light' and allowed it to re-join with its other half 'The Darkness.' This one action had cut of their ability to spread through the minds of all other creatures and whoever did that would suffer as much as 'The Slayer'. The Slayer was here, The Slayer was their priority and they could all now smell the blood of the Esmer Alder on her, they could follow the scent easily now, they would track down and kill The Slayer.

The female human was within their grasp but they themselves had to find it in their own form. This Sarah Human would suffer and die and then a new queen would rise from one of them, that was how it worked, it was proper and right. After they had dispensed with the Human they would recapture the light and the dark, return calm to their hive. It was time to swarm and so they left their caves, swarming out into the light of two Suns that they had not seen for two thousand

CHAPTER FOURTEEN

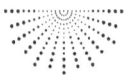

The Minotaur's eyes flamed red as he came to the surface reluctantly and churlishly spatting back at the Agent. "I have no love for the suns or the ground above, I have no love of the creatures that live above ground but know this Human, I have a pure hatred of all that is wrong and these Alder creatures from underground are utterly wrong.

They are from before my time, they are a spawn of evil and can never be anything else. All are at war with them and these creatures must not be able to travel to other worlds, we must eradicate them all." His muscles tightened in readiness for the fight ahead.

The Minotaur then stepped into the light of day and lay Robin's tortured body down on the ground in the warmth of the suns, in the hope that he may heal a bit. He knelt down and cupped his huge hand scooping water up from the river and poured it over Robin's wounds. He poured some into Robin's mouth and the boy swallowed instinctively but without opening his eyes.

The Agent laid Kobalos' tiny form down next to Robin's limp body, standing next to the impossibly huge creature, he paused and thought for a long moment. As he lifted his head he slightly adjusted the two swords strapped to his back then straightened his suit and tie, after all appearance was very important, even when at war.

"If I cannot return to my brother, Minotaur, then there is nothing else left for me but to help others here, that is my only logic. There are too many variables for me to understand in this world, so I shall follow your wisdom and ask you to be my new Commander in Chief. That means 'Please tell me what to do and I shall do it.' Is that okay with you?"

The Minotaur stopped for a moment to understand this strange Human and looked at it with curiosity. He could sense the Human's confusion, then said in a more friendly, softer voice. "Yes Human, I can do that."

. . .

The pair watched the beginning of the swarm. Luckily, they had come to the surface into the creek some way off from Dargal's cave. From this distance they were able to watch safely but with morbid fascination as hundreds upon hundreds of the Alder spewed out from every orifice, cave opening, crevice and crack into the canyon next to Dargal's home. Sniffing the air deeply the Alder headed down along the walls and floor of the pass in one single direction, away from the caves, the Minotaur and the Agent.

The Minotaur picked Robin up and said to the Agent. "We will make our war with them soon enough but first we must take Kobalos to his people." He turned to go and then stopped, looked round at the Agent and said. "Pick up Kobalos and follow me, it is not far."

The Agent did as he was told and then a very strange thing happened for the Agent, he felt, he actually felt something, something very small and it was 'gratitude'.

CHAPTER FIFTEEN

The arrow swished over John's head almost parting his hair it was so close and flew straight into the Spiderbird that had been closing in on him from behind. The eight leggy bird squealed as it dropped to the ground. Several other Spiderbirds flapped their wings and headed away from the back of John with their legs dangling pointlessly. To John they looked just like daddy long legs but way bigger and much scarier.

He turned to see the injured Spiderbird hit the ground, then he spotted the Jasban hurtling up from the creek towards him.

The Jasban passed John and Dargal at great speed, smashing through small trees and crushing plants as he went, heading up gleefully to his brother. Despite everything that had happened or needed to happen next, he shouted out into his brother's and everyone else's minds. 'Brother, my brother you are back! Who wants to play jump, or let's go do the Electric Daisy leap, or let's chase Cratalorg, my brother is back!'

Rachel slid down from her Jasban and thought to him. 'Looks like someone is pleased to see you!' But the bigger Jasban didn't answer her, he just drooled his happiness then sped off down the Ravine to meet his brother. As they crashed into each other with a body slam, the feeling of joy and relief that they felt reached everyone. With claws in pads out they rolled along the ravine smashing through flora and fauna as they went. The younger one thought out. 'Where did you go? I had no one to beat at 'Jump', it's been mad here, where did you go?'

The bigger Jasban jumped onto his brother. 'You were too slow little brother so I went to find a bigger challenge in the Human's world. That's a strange place for sure!'

The younger Jasban retorted. 'I always said you were good with the idiot ones!' They both dribbled and drooled with happiness and relief at finding each other alive. Then ran around in circles to body slam each other once more.

. . .

Kate looked to the sisters. "There's two of them?" Rachel and Sarah laughed.

It was a moment of joy in this dark time that everyone shared. Everyone, even Dargal smiled. As the two Jasban started talking and finding out about each other's Journeys, Sarah put her arm out to Rachel and lifted her up onto Brian's back. They trotted with Kate running behind, down to meet John and Dargal and, Sarah noted, a Frab?

When the groups met John felt suddenly awkward, being confronted by three females of different ages and all three looking as hard as nails. Oh, and an actual Unicorn. "Hello." he said nervously "Thank you for not killing me. Unicorns exist? Why am I not surprised? What was that thing behind me?"

Sarah slid down off Brian and took her time to answer as she walked around John whilst looking him up and down. "Spiderbird." she said sizing him up. "Useless predators, they're still evolving into meat eaters so they have a few thousand years until they are a proper threat. Last time we saw you, you were strangling one of my best friends."

. . .

John was confused at first but then cottoned on. "Oh, Robin you mean? Yes, sorry about that, I had a weird thing in my head that sort of took me over. How did you see that?"

All three females looked at him expectantly and his feeling of uncomfortableness increased. "I didn't kill him if that's what you're thinking, honestly!" Then he thought to himself, but too loudly. 'How the hell do they know about that?'

Sarah thought back. 'Because Rachel has a bucket.'

Dargal hit Sarah's leg. "Well 'Sarah the Adventurer', what have you to say for yourself eh?"

Sarah realised that she had forgotten Dargal and gasped an apology. "Dargal! Oh! I am so glad to see you my old friend, what are you doing with this?" Then pointed at John who was beginning to regret coming to find help.

Dargal looked up at John with a slow look and then said "Don't give him too hard a time Sarah, he has proved himself to be a friend. Now give me a hug, we need to catch up."

. . .

Despite the oncoming storm of monsters Sarah sat down crossed legged as Dargal walked forward and they embraced, her eyes glazed over for a moment as she caught up with his memories and a montage of images flashed through her mind. Sarah breathed deeply and thought to him. 'You think Robin is alive, don't you?'

Dargal frowned. 'I have heard that roar before Sarah. If he was there then the boy has a chance, I think.'

Sarah smiled. "You are still hiding the 'Pen Trick' in your mind from me Dargal, show it to me please, don't I deserve to see how you do it?"

Dargal beamed a mischievous smile and thought back 'When and if this is over, I promise. Now stand up, you look too small down here and we have much to do. Did you and Jack leave the back up in place before you left? Because we are really going to need it. The Alder are coming for you, they are many more than an attack of Cratalorg, and they are even more vicious and nasty than a Hungry White Tiger on a bad day!'

. . .

Sarah stood and thought down to Dargal. 'Of course we did, I just have to get back up there and set them off at the right time. I wasn't expecting so many enemies, might we need more help?'

Dargal nodded and said out loud. "From what I have seen there are hundreds of these creatures that are heading here fast, so we must hurry and have…" There he stopped abruptly and stared past Sarah directly at Rachel. "Oh, my stars! You are Rachel aren't you. Rachel the Intrepid!"

Rachel was a bit taken aback but remained polite. "Yes sir, I am, and you are Dargal Sarah tells me?"

Dargal beamed. "Yes, I am Rachel, now you just sit down and cross your legs like you saw your sister do because I need to say hello properly."

Rachel looked at Sarah who nodded at her, Rachel seemed a tad confused but did as she was asked. Lowering herself to the floor, she sat cross legged as Dargal walked over and put his tiny arms around her, well, as much of her as he could. As he did so he thought to her. 'Hold on Rachel this will be bumpy.' A flood of images swept through her mind, images of Sarah's adventures in this world where Dargal had been involved. A wave of emotions simultaneously exploded into Rachels young mind. Memories of Dargal and Sarah's history, of him being released from the Witch, she couldn't help but grin from ear to ear. To see her sister's past life flash before her, as well as Dargal's own life was overwhelming. She put her arms around Dargal and squeezed him in a bear hug for a whole silent 20 seconds.

Right there and then she grew up, without losing her sense of fun, that she would always hold onto. Sarah was right, she did love Dargal.

John looked at Sarah and said. "Are they okay? Only there's this swarm of bad creatures coming and…"

Sarah put her finger to John's lips to stop him from talking and thought out to him. 'Some things are worth risking being late for. This will be over shortly.'

Dargal let loose of Rachel, as they parted Rachel looked into his eyes, she didn't need to speak any words but just smiled her thank you to him and gave a small nod. She had tears in her eyes but now they were tears of Joy. Dargal went and climbed up onto a small friendly looking boulder and grinned to himself.

Rachel looked up at her sister. "I think I understand you a bit more now Sarah, I am so lucky to have you as my sister."

Sarah just smiled at her and nodded in understanding. "A hug from a Dwarf is a bit special though isn't it eh?"

Rachel nodded and smiled like she had never smiled before, despite everything. Shaking her head, she attempted to make sense of everything that was now filling her mind.

Dargal stood back. "Right then, we have a storm of evil coming to kill Sarah and we have to find the idiot boy. Best we get to work Sarah, eh? We are only ahead of them because the Jasban is such a fast runner but they will be here in minutes."

Clara interrupted the moment and thought out. 'Clara has been told by Moley that Sarah is a great Warrior! Sarah help Robin yes?'

. . .

Sarah looked at the Rock that Dargal was now sitting on. 'Clara Frab! You were there when I killed the Witch weren't you? I remember you. Moley gave you your name, didn't she?"

Clara unfurled herself as Dargal slid down off of her back. 'Yes, I am Clara Frab and Robin is my friend, he save Clara Frab and Robin need help now.'

Sarah could feel the love for Robin in Clara's thoughts. 'Robin is my friend too Clara, but first we have to fight off the Alder so that I can get us out of this Ravine alive and find him. Will you help us?'

Clara stood to her full height slowly. To everyone's utter astonishment she began speaking out loud, although in stilted sentences and her voice trilled. "Clara Frab help Sarah to fight bad creatures. Then we save Robin boy yes?"

Sarah smiled at Robin's new friend and spoke out loud to her. "Yes Clara Frab, yes, but if we all die fighting the Alder then at least Robin might know that we died trying to save him okay?"

. . .

Clara Frab nodded and then looked out behind herself. 'They are here!'

The first of the Alder appeared at the entrance of the main tunnel, which lead up to the creek from Dargal's home.

Sarah looked at Clara thinking out to her and putting some images into Clara's head. 'Best we be quick then. Can you reach any other Frab with your thoughts, we may need their help?'

Clara just looked at Sarah, for a moment she tried to understand the new images in her head. Images of a boulder, a net, spikes and other images that Clara frowned at, trying to understand them and thought back. 'Frab exhausted from Dragon fire.'

Sarah spoke into Clara's mind once more. 'Ok, there is another friend out there somewhere, that, if you could find him and tell him I need help would make a huge difference to us all.' At that she projected one last image into Clara's mind. Clara stalled.

. . .

She looked down at Sarah confused and spoke from her mind only to Sarah. 'But creature bad, even Frab fear creature, Sarah sure?'

Sarah walked forward, put out her hand and placed it in Clara's. She spoke softly. 'Frab need not fear this creature if Frab helping Sarah, Sarah promise.'

Clara gripped Sarah's tiny hand for a moment, nodded, turned and ran down the Ravine directly towards the enemy. As she chose a path in her mind she jumped, curled in her arms and legs becoming a rock, well more a boulder now, hurtling through the Ravine at great speed.

She became a rolling danger that nothing could stop and sped on down and into the bottom of the Creek. As she reached them the Alder just parted to let her through not knowing what devastation she may be able to bring them. A falling rock was of no concern to them.

Sarah then shouted out to everyone. "Back up to my place, as quick as you can now."

. . .

Kate was confused. "You want us to hide from these things in your cave, behind a curtain of Vines?"

"No Kate, we can't hide from these things, this Ravine is my home, all of it, mine and Jacks. We knew right from the beginning that the Witch might send her puppets to attack us, so we prepared. Jack always said 'have a backup plan,' and whilst we weren't expecting this, we do have a few tricks up our sleeves! We have no choice but to kill them, all of them. If what I understand is true then they won't stop until I am dead and even when I am, I don't think that they will just go away. This is where you have to trust me Kate."

Rachel frowned and Kate shook her head. "I trust you Sarah. I may have no magic but I do have my training. You impress me at every turn young lady and I'm right behind you!" She looked behind her at the approaching swarm, now just a kilometre or so behind them and drew her sword.

The first Jasban got the message and thought out to his brother. 'Right then! Let's go. I'll take Rachel, you lift Kate the new human okay?'

. . .

Sarah Jumped up onto Brian and put her hand out to John. "You'll need a lift I think, pick Dargal up, two steps and bounce on your left foot then jump to mount okay?"

John took Sarah's hand as Brian began to trot and did as instructed. In a flash he found himself sitting on the back of a Unicorn with a Dwarf standing between him and Sarah. "Thank you for not killing me." He was beginning to realise why Robin was devoted to this girl, she was something else!

Sarah frowned to herself and looked at her companions all heading back up the Ravine. The Alder cautiously sniffed around like hound dogs. They were seeking the Slayer, they were many, they were strong, they were powerful. As Brian galloped on, Sarah thought a private thought to the oncoming swarm. 'Bring it on Monsters, you have found me but I have waited for this moment all my life! It is my fault that I killed your Queen but she was mad and as evil as you are and I will not allow you to hurt my friends. I am very hard to kill, bring it on!'

CHAPTER SIXTEEN

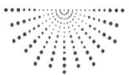

The Kobaloi were waiting as the Minotaur strode towards their home. The Agent was confused. "Why are we heading into the wall?" He asked as they headed away from the river at the bottom of the creek towards the huge wall of rock that rose up to the surface of the planet.

The Minotaur was not used to conversation but had learned over a couple of thousand years that other creatures were curious. Not everyone could wait for an answer to present itself, some had to continuously ask about what might happen next.

He had stopped being annoyed about that after his friend, Theseus, had said to him. "We Humans do not have the complete understanding of things that you seem to have. We have become 'apart' from nature, so we are constantly trying to get back to understanding by asking questions. The question that us 'Humans' don't ask ourselves is. "Why do we think that, because we are not a part of nature, that we are better than it?" We are a part of Nature, whether we believe it or not. We live our lives asking pointless questions instead of just being part of nature." Theseus was the very first Human that the Minotaur was impressed by and after him very few Humans met his match in understanding anything.

The wall in the side of the Creek the Agent was referring to looked like it was entirely covered in fur and feathers. The Minotaur was heading towards it like it was a flimsy curtain that he could just walk through. Whilst it looked like it would be soft to lean against it still looked solid. When the Minotaur carrying Robin and the agent carrying Kobalos were just a few feet from the wall, the wall itself collapsed, dropping like a beaded curtain, falling in tiny parts.

It seemed to fall from a hundred feet above them like a fast flowing downward moving tsunami that would in seconds engulf them both. The Minotaur turned to his companion saying in his loud, deep, growling voice. "You have nothing to fear human. Stand still now and let this happen."

The Agent stopped moving but held Kobalos protectively in his arms. An emotion niggled at his usually emotionless mind which made him hold Kobalos even tighter, it was an odd feeling that he reasoned might be what a parent protecting its child might feel like. What was odder, was that he felt a feeling.

The wall fell like water upon them both and yet The

Agent felt nothing as he was engulfed by this mass of fur and feathers and hands and feet crawling all over him. He could see nothing and could barely breathe as his senses became overloaded. The creatures that had made up the wall whirled around him tugging lightly at Kobalos' small body. He managed one muffled shout out. "Minotaur! What do I do?"

The Minotaur spoke back unusually gently. "Let them take Kobalos Human. He belongs to them, they are Kobaloi, older and wiser even than me."

The agent looked down through the storm of feathers at the tiny being in his arms. Another emotion came to him, he was sad. Stopping within the chaos for several moments as a tear came to his eye, ran down his nose and dropped onto Kobalos. He was so surprised, never in his entire life had he shed a tear before today. "I am sorry Sprite. I am so sorry that I may have killed you."

As he said this the storm around him slowed and the Agent released his grip holding Kobalos' tiny body aloft. The storm whirled again as it lifted Kobalos from the Agent. As he rose into the air the tiny being began to sparkle, with crackles of light emanating from beneath his clothing. Kobalos' eyes slowly began opening, looking at the Agent he smiled kindly. "Learn now cold Human one, learn and become warm!" and with that Kobalos was lifted from the Agents arms and disappeared into the storm of fur and feathers.

The Agent stepped back at the same time as the Minotaur, moving out of the storm and back towards the creek. "Walk backwards Human and watch. As I am to you, these creatures are to me. They tell me what to do, they give me purpose, Kobalos is a part of them."

Both Agent and Minotaur walked slowly backwards, watching as the storm raged out over and above them, carrying Kobalos in their hurricane. As the pair continued backward the storm seemed to slow and became a cloud of colour that then slowed even further. It formed into the shape of an enormous kind of bird, but heavier and with more limbs than any bird should rightly have. The Agent also thought that no bird should have the head of a Lion, yet this one did.

The Kobaloi melded together and became a new form, a new being, or at least an older being. One that was more powerful than other beings, wiser, more compassionate and more than just the sum of its parts. The Kobaloi became a Griffin that took to the air, it was vast, it filled the sky above them stretched and tested its wings.

The Minotaur laid the unconscious Robin down before the Griffin on the shores of the river, stepped back, kneeled down and looked up. "It is good to see you again after all this time Master. I have to tell you, although you will already know, that this world is under a dark and dangerous threat the like of which even I have never seen. The Alder have awoken."

The Griffin heard the Minotaur and glided gracefully to the Creek nearby and spoke into his mind. The Agent heard the conversation and something in him was moved. There was something about the respect, the ancient nobility that there was in the relationship between servant and Master. The Agent was beginning to think that not all of 'The Gift' had left him.

The eyes of the Griffin sparkled as its mind spoke out. 'We are glad to see you again Minotaur, you have served us well over the years, despite the recently broken Portals.'

The Minotaur knelt and snorted with anger and shame. "The Alder took my mind, but even so I crushed only those vessels that had, as yet, no life in them."

The Griffin settled itself before the Minotaur then bowed its majestic head. 'We felt your struggle through Kobalos, we have felt this danger coming for a long time Minotaur.'

The Minotaur felt relieved and the Agent could feel it. 'I must do what I can to stop the swarm and to save a friend, yet I must ask a favour. This Human boy has served you without knowing it, he and his Mother and Father before him have served this world well. He has more strength in his heart than his youthfulness knows. He is yours to help or deny, I need to go to help fight a war with the enemy called 'The Alder'.

The Griffin lifted its wings, almost touching the ground like a swimmer slowly treading water, almost touching the ground it hovered and looked down at the boy. Its low deep voice reverberated through the chasm, along the creek and through the valleys around. 'We are awakened to right a wrong, Kobalos lives and we thank you for that but your enemy is ancient. The Alder are not like anything that we have seen before. They are ancient and have no place in this world or any other.'

The Griffin came down gently to land at the shore next to Robin. "Minotaur, you know that we never interfere as all species must co-exist here, yet we understand that this is unusual, this is an anomaly."

The Minotaur stood, sweeping his arms out and bowing in supplication. Raising his head, he looked up at the most powerful creature in any present universe. "You were awakened to save Kobalos, that you have done. Whether you help us to kill off this infection of creatures from your domain or not, is your choice Griffin. Help the creatures in this world or don't, I only serve you as I can. I have survived their attack against me and the Portals that I make for you."

The Minotaur stepped forward and looked up at the head of the Griffin. "Know this my Lord, I leave you to help save a Human child, she is as worthy of saving as the creatures in this world. We have both nurtured them over so many centuries, and now this child lays before you. What you do is your choice, but my choice is to go to war, I go to do what I believe is right, what you do is up to your conscience."

The Minotaur didn't wait for a response from its Master, he grabbed the Agent by his shoulder. "Walk beside me now. We go to save Sarah the Adventurer from the Witches brood but if we can't we will die trying."

The Agent stood and nodded. He 'felt' that he had an actual purpose, he 'felt' that he might be able to help, more importantly he 'felt' something and feeling anything was very new. He followed the Minotaur, the impossible creature who was twice his height and size. They walked with purpose, back into the Creek, towards the Ravine. The Agent stopped for a second and looked back at the mighty Griffin standing proudly, he sent back towards it a thought. 'You were right Kobalos, I feel. Thank you.' Then he turned back to follow his Commander in Chief, The Minotaur and asked. "What now Minotaur?"

The Minotaur was angry and barked back. "Now we go to war Human. I do not expect you to live for long, but know that I believe you are an exceptional human. I do not say that lightly. I hope that I am wrong about how long you will live but our enemy are deadly." With that he strode towards the Ravine and to war. The Agent followed without questioning his commander in Chief any more.

CHAPTER SEVENTEEN

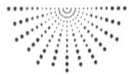

The voice of the Alder rasped into everyone's minds as it smelt the smell of the slayer in the air as it crawled up the Ravine. It was full of joy knowing that soon it would have payback. 'We have found you at last Sarah the Adventurer, we have found you child and we will kill you slowly so that we can feed more plentifully. You killed our Queen, you betrayed her and now we are coming for you. Don't resist us child, you know your life belongs to us. We are ancient beyond this world, faster, stronger and more powerful than any other species.' The voice of the Alder softened, yet somehow sounded more menacing. 'You know that we will kill you eventually and we will do it slowly child, why struggle, we can end your pain quickly, just come to us now.'

Rachel shivered at the voice in her head and felt fear. She looked back down the Ravine from the back of the Jasban as he bounded up towards the surface. They were still a good fifteen minutes away from the meadow at full pelt. She looked forwards towards Sarah and shouted. "We're not going to make it Sarsy, they're catching up fast!"

Sarah responded without turning around. "We aren't heading to the surface Rach, just get to that boulder ahead and make sure that you are behind it, you too Kate." Kate was a Government Agent and just listened, she was used to taking orders, just not from someone so young.

Within a few seconds both Jasban had passed the boulder. Kate halted hers and slid down from his back. Running towards the boulder to see what Sarah was doing and if she could help.

Sarah jumped nimbly to the ground leaving John on Brian's back saying to him. "Wait here, I'll be just a minute."

John looked around and said "Right, whatever, have you seen these things that are hunting you before by the way? Have you seen how big and evil they are? They're twice the size of us, have vicious looking tentacles covering the backs of them and their eyes, their eyes are something else, all black and huge and their legs are on backwards and..."

Sarah just said into John's mind. 'Shhh, calm yourself. Yes, I have seen the Alder, I saw them when the Witch took me to show me off to them as a Trophy when I was a small child. She wanted to leave them, to grow past being their Queen and to become a Human. I had a Bucket and I was a female but I was too young for her to use, because of that she grew to hate me. The Alder hate me for many reasons John but mainly because their Queen betrayed them and they blame me! I killed her and they want me dead.'

John was overwhelmed by events at this point. He'd had enough of thinking, he was ready to just help where he could. 'Hopefully I will live through this and we can sit down whilst you tell me what all of that means?'

Sarah responded. 'It means I've known that this day was coming, so Jack and I got prepared!' As she picked up a tiny hammer lying next to the bottom of the boulder.

She paused, looked Kate in the eye and said. "Always have a backup plan!" As she turned she smiled knowingly. She swung the tiny hammer, dislodging three tiny pebbles away from in front of the huge rock. Brian knelt down to make it faster for her to remount, Sarah leapfrogged onto his back. Brian stood up to his full height, setting off as quickly as he could up the hill away from the approaching danger.

Kate ran back to the Jasban and leapt up onto his back thinking down to him. 'How long have you known this girl Jasban?'

The Jasban drooled. 'Sarah the adventurer?' He gurgled with pleasure in his thoughts. 'For a tiny life time and forever, she is awesome for a human!'

As he said this more pebbles started rolling away from under the boulder, then larger rocks started to move away in a cascade. Within seconds the mighty boulder itself was released and started to hurtle down the Ravine.

Kate shouted down to her. "That is impressive Sarah but one Boulder against a horde? The kill rate is small!"

Sarah smiled to herself and shouted back. "Jack called this 'The Pinball Defence', just watch." Kate turned as the huge boulder gained speed and crashed into the stump of a tree, the boulder changed direction hurtling to hit another boulder and that boulder started its descent down the ravine. The incline was steep here, within seconds it hit another boulder way to the left which in turn rolled further down the ravine hitting two more boulders that were side by side. The cascade developed quickly now, it was like an avalanche of snow, gaining momentum as more and more stones, rocks and boulders joined in the descent. The tidal wave of destruction caught the Alder by surprise, devastating the enemy hoard in vast numbers, crushing and pounding them to death. They had been racing up the Ravine in pursuit of Sarah with such fury that they hadn't seen the danger approaching. The sound was horrific and yet somehow oddly pleasing to the girls.

The remaining Alder saw the devastation coming toward them and started climbing up along the walls of the Ravine, racing on towards the Slayer using the trees that grew from the sides of the ravine as purchase to avoid being crushed.

Kate shouted over the mayhem. "When did you set this trap Sarah?"

Sarah looked back. "When I was 10 years old. The Witch hated me even then. Jack wanted to keep me safe from whatever she might have thrown at us so we made the pebble cascade and other stuff. It'll slow them down but not for long, we have to get higher up."

Brian galloped on, further up the Ravine with Kate and Rachel following on the Jasbans. John leaned back into Sarah. "You have seen these creatures before? You must have known how huge and nasty they are; how can you fight them?"

Sarah thought back to him. 'I saw these monsters when I was seven years old, when the witch took me to her home. We have a history, me and these things. You are new here aren't you John? Watch and learn Kid!' John smarted from being called Kid and suddenly realised how annoyed Robin must have felt being called that.

The Alder continued their assault despite losing many of their number to the crushing rock. The swarm was intent on its purpose of killing the slayer, a new queen would rise and breed to replenish their numbers. The rest of the swarm continued its ascent along the steep walls of the Ravine in pursuit of the Slayer, of Sarah.

The troupe came to the burnt-out tree. Sarah shouted to Rachel. "Climb up to the top Rach, there's a hollow and a lot more arrows up there than we can carry, just keep firing at them high into the air, hopefully some will hit their target."

Rachel jumped down from The Jasban and did as her sister asked. When she had climbed to the top, she found that she was in a natural turret that had water, as well as fresh fruit growing inside. Rachel ignored these and swung her bow round, lifted arrows one by one from the stacked quivers and started nocking and launching them into the air.

The first two bounced off rocks and Sarah shouted up.

"Take it slowly Rach, concentrate like I showed you." Rachel drew an arrow slowly and nocked it to her bow, she breathed slowly, calming herself. She then thought of Brian as she drew back the dropweed string on her bow, her eyes flamed bright blue. She felt that familiar strength of Unicorn flowing through her veins, her eyes narrowed in concentration as she searched out her targets.

She aimed high allowing for the drop and loosed the arrow which whizzed through the air and found its mark far down the Ravine. It pierced straight through the huge black eye of an Alder and out of the back of its skull. The creature stopped dead as its brain ceased functioning, it fell to the floor with a loud 'thwap', lifeless and unmoving. Rachel nodded to herself and slowly drew another arrow then shouted out. "I had the Witch in my head, she was vile and evil. I have a Unicorn's magic in my head now, that is the right feeling for me. These Alder need to DIE!"

John looked up to Rachel. 'You had one in your mind as well?'

Rachel looked down at John from her vantage point. "Yes. The Witch made me her slave; she was one of them. I'd still be a slave of hers if Robin hadn't helped me break free from the grip of her mind."

Sarah shouted up to the turret. "Nice shot Sis!" As she jumped down from Brian she pointed to the base of the tree at a leather bag. "Kate, open that bag, take out the scratcher and the Frow wool. There are some oil-soaked rags at the bottom in a bowl, just spin the scratcher round a few times and it should light the wool. We need a flame so I can dip my arrows in oil and fire.

Kate shook her head as she suddenly realised who was in charge here. Kate did exactly as she was asked to do. She opened the bag and found what Sarah had called 'the scratcher' to be a small tube-like cylindrical drum made of a rough granite. It had a handle at the end of it and with a row of flints attached. She put the wool in front as Sarah reached down and grabbed an oil-soaked rag, tore off a strip then wrapped it around the tip of an arrow.

Kate wound the handle around and as she did so a spray of sparks flew into the wool setting it instantly alight. "Who made this thing Sarah? It is amazingly effective and so simple!"

Sarah knocked her arrow and put it down into the flame. "That's one of mine Kate, I just made a bigger version of Jack's petrol lighter, I saw him use once before we came here." Without pausing she lifted her bow with its flaming arrow, looked down the Ravine, aimed at the left side of the rocky walls, waited for a few seconds as she watched the Alder hurtling up towards them, loosed her arrow then thought out. 'Burn parasites, burn!'

She didn't wait to see if it hit its mark but turned back took another small oily rag, wrapped it around the tip of a fresh arrow and setting it alight aimed to the right side, loosed it and this time stood to watch the effect.

As the first arrow hit its mark a wall of flame erupted along the left side, rapidly engulfing the trees. As the fire raced along the ravine wall it set alight row upon row of oil-soaked branches and dry wood. This trap had been laid by Jack and Sarah years before. Hundreds of Alder screamed in surprise and pain as they were caught in the inferno, the remaining Alder fell back from this new enemy of fire.

The centre of the Ravine was, as yet, untouched by the flames. Any Alder not burned or crushed by rocks began racing up the valley like tentacled raptors shouting out their rage into everyone's minds. 'Kill as many of us as you can humans, we are still coming for you. We will find you and kill you, you cannot escape us Slayer, we are many!'

On hearing the voice in her head Sarah looked around at her sister, Kate, John, Dargal, the Jasban and Brian and said into all of their minds. 'This is not your fight my friends, please find somewhere safe, this is going to get nasty.' Without waiting for an answer, she started walking directly towards the Alder. They beasts saw her approaching, they crawled and ran towards her, around the fires that burned brightly and over the dead bodies of their swarm. Despite having killed many of their number with her traps, more Alder were arriving at the bottom of the Ravine and joining the throng.

Rachel shouted out to her sister. "No Sarah! No, you can't face them alone! Sarah, please no, I can't lose you again, please!"

On hearing Rachel's cry of anguish, Kate, John and Dargal looked at each other and with no words ran to Sarah's side with swords in hand. Kate shouted up to Rachel. "Stay where you are Rach and cover us!" Rachel nodded and though her arms were tired from firing arrows at the enemy she gathered more arrows ready to loose. She knew that was what she could do, not much against a swarm, it would be more like an annoying gnat than any real threat, but it was how she could help right now.

John thought out to Sarah. "I know Robin loves you Sarah, he is so much cooler than I first thought, I really hope he is alive.'

Sarah frowned. "How do you know Robin loves me? He has never said that to me."

Robin looked at her in mild astonishment. "Really! He is only here because of you. He might have just died, giving his life for you, I didn't know you until this day but even I am amazed by you kid, um, Sarah! Robin is utterly devoted to you; how can you be so amazing and not have seen that?"

Sarah just stared at John and then looked down at the floor. "I really hope we all live through this." Then as she looked out at the creatures coming towards them she spoke softly. "I'd really like to see him again."

John put his hand on her shoulder. "You should know, he might be an idiot at times but he is utterly devoted to you for sure."

Sarah stared back for a moment, taking everything that John had said into her mind and smiled. "If he is alive, I will find him. Thank you, John."

Brian and the Jasban were already by Sarah's side as Brian thought out to the group. "If we let them take Sarah then each of us will lose. They will become stronger again with a new queen, a new Esmer Alder. We cannot let Sarah die because if we do we all lose, do you understand me Sarah, this is not just your fight, this is every creature in this world and beyond's fight.'

He looked around at the others to make sure they were listening as he continued. 'If Sarah dies then these creatures get to rule our whole world. They have been awakened and will cause pain to everyone, everywhere and for all time. We cannot let them take Sarah for any reason!'

Dargal looked up at Sarah. "Looks like we're all in this together Sarah." He raised his sword into the air. "So as Jack would say 'To death, Sarah or glory!'"

Sarah looked around at her companions. "Okay then, together." Looking down at the ascending horror of the Alder, she pointed down the ravine. "Rach, from where you are can you see a red disc just above the Electric Daisies down there?"

Rachel peered out from her vantage point, along the walls of the Ravine and eventually spotted her target. "Yeah, got it!"

Sarah turned to Brian but thought into Rachel's mind. 'Imagine that it is Robin's face and keep firing arrows at it until it turns yellow. Can you do that sis?' Rachel smiled and nodded as she thought of Robin.

He had picked her up and saved her from the Dragons when they first came here together. He had saved her from the Witch, she shivered for a moment then her eyes flashed a brighter blue and she started loosing her arrows at the large disc with surprising speed and accuracy. She realised in that moment that she actually loved her older friend Robin who had saved her so many times. Each arrow that found its mark knocked the disc back an inch or so.

Sarah turned back to Brian. "I always thought that this was my fault. The Witch told me that if she failed it was my fault and everyone would suffer because of me. Are you telling me that this is not all my fault, I mean she came to our world because of me, she hurt people just to get back at me, how is this not my fault?"

Brian whinnied and spun around in a circle. 'This has never been your fault Sarah the Adventurer! I am shocked that you have carried that belief with you all these years. She went to your world to increase her power, that had nothing to do with you. You are a good human and always have been, the Witch was an evil thing!' He walked over to her and stood proudly before her. 'I am so sorry that I didn't see your pain, you were never at fault Sarah the Adventurer, not ever!'

Sarah put her hand to her mouth in real surprise and shock. A tear fell from her eye, then she stroked Brian's muzzle. 'Thank you, Brian, thank you!' Looking down for just a second whilst that sank in, it sank in deeply. She realised, what everyone else had known all along, she was not a bad person, this was not her fault. A new feeling came over her, she felt angry. The Witch had tricked her, manipulated her, used her! Well now that was going to change, now it was payback time!

She took a deep breath at this revelation, it was like a curse being lifted from her. She looked at the enemy rapidly approaching and thought out to everyone. 'Right then, not my fault.' Nodding to herself as she breathed in deeply and thought for a few moments more. 'Right then, time to kill off these parasites, if we can. If we can't then thank you people for being my friends!' To herself she repeated over and over. 'Not my fault! Not my fault....'

From seemingly nowhere an Alder stood up behind Sarah and struck her down with its backwards pointed elbow, its tentacles began wrapping around her, slicing into her skin to cause her as much pain as it could to feed upon!

Sarah screamed in pain and surprise but as soon as the Alder rose up from its hiding place Brian had leapt to impale it with his Alicorn. His aim was precise, spearing directly into the centre of the creatures back from which its sharp tentacles reached out towards Sarah. He raised his head lifting the cruel creature into the air. With tentacles flailing in distress and shock the Alder dropped Sarah to the ground. Brian spun round, causing the Alder to slide off his spiked Alicorn. John and Dargal immediately joined the attack, slicing off its tentacles and stabbing it to death.

John was shaking as he looked at the beast and then at Dargal. "These things are terrifying but you are very scary for a small person?"

Dargal smiled back. "Thank you human."

Brian thought down to Sarah 'Are you okay? Alive even?'

Sarah groaned. 'I'm okay Brian, I think….' She curled up in pain. 'Not too much damage.' But blood dripped from her midriff belying her words.

Their attention was drawn to Rachel's sudden shout of success as her arrows turned the disc to yellow. "Look!" she shouted pointing to the Ravine. The group wheeled round just as a huge number of the creatures were swept up in a net. It was attached to the arm of an enormous and well disguised Trebuchet, which now swung its wooden arm up flinging the hapless creatures high into the air. With tentacles flailing and screams of surprise they landed back down in the creek with a thud. It was a move that none of the monsters would survive. Dargal looked at Sarah somewhat annoyed. "So that's where Jack hid them!" He looked up at Sarah and barked at her. "So, where's the other one?"

Sarah looked at Dargal a tad guiltily whilst trying not to bleed too much. "Ummmmm." With a guilty look on her face she watched the Ravine as a second wooden arm sprung into the air, repeating the same action as the last. It surprised another huge number of Alder who were caught in the second net, then found themselves hurtling into the air and down to their deaths against the rocks in the creek below. "You mean that one?"

Dargal just shook his head in disbelief.

Rachel shouted down from her vantage point. "Sarah, there's more of them!" Sure enough more Alder began swarming their way into the Ravine and up towards Sarah and her friends. "How many more are there Sarah, I am getting really tired now!" Sarah looked up at her amazing younger sister, she could see the bright blue in her eyes begin to dull.

The trees in the lower part of the Ravine were burning an inferno of heat. Still the Alder advanced, all be it more slowly and cautiously now.

Kate shouted over to Sarah. "This is a swarm Sarah; we can't fight a swarm, can we?"

Sarah looked deadly serious. "No, we can't Kate but we do have to 'Exterminate' them. If we don't stop them, they will take this world and all of the creatures in it! Now is just us against them."

She lifted up her sword, shook her head to clear the pain from it, glanced at the oncoming swarm then shouted out. "I'm sorry!" Looking to her friends, the Unicorn, who had taught her so much and given her unusual strengths. The Jasban, who had played with her and her long gone friend White Tiger. Her beautiful, amazing little sister who would stop at nothing and give up everything to save her older sister.

She looked at John the ingenious, who looked exhausted and bewildered by everything. Finally, she looked at Dargal, her oldest friend in this troupe and knew that they might all die here together. "Jack and I set the traps but we didn't know how strong or how many our enemies would be. Looks like we fell short."

Everyone looked at Sarah with expectation and she looked back at them with sorrow. "I have nothing left, that is all the traps we set. We both thought that they would be enough. Now we have to fight them with the weapons that we hold and nothing else, apart from this last thing that is."

Kate looked down at the swarm of monsters heading their way then back at Sarah. "If you were anyone else Sarah, I would say you were mad. What can we few do against that horde, have you really no traps or tricks left?"

Sarah looked out at her friends and down at the enemy. They were only about half a kilometre away now and getting closer by the second. "Only one Kate, after that we are on our own. We may be few in number but these things don't seem too smart, evil and nasty yes but they're not very clever, so that is our weapon. We have to outsmart them and so let's start with this!"

Sarah walked over to a hanging vine. "Your sword John, may I?" Her politeness was at odds with the danger they were in, John handed his weapon over without a word. Sarah took the sword, raised it in the air then swung it at the vine.

As it was cut the vine spun up into the air as if it had been holding back a heavy weight. The troupe watched in awe as vine after vine twisted, snapped then flew. Eventually, they reached the two unusually square patches of Electric Daisies. Mayhem ensued as the fields of daisies on either side of the Ravine were flung into the air directly at the oncoming swarm.

As the flowers hit the Alder, they exploded in a mass of crackling electricity and sparkling light. The troupe watched on in stunned silence as Alder after Alder dropped to the ground never to rise again. The rest of the Swarm faltered then dropped back as it tried to understand what had just happened.

The Jasban turned to his younger brother. "Glad I didn't drop into that patch little brother!" Both Jasban made a very strange sound, one that is, of a Jasban sniggering, it sounded just like a Raven drowning!

The brothers looked at Kate who was hiding her eyes, then up at Rachel expectantly. Rachel knew it was time to retreat from her tree tower. She sent off one last volley of arrows, trying to reduce the numbers of the enemy stalking them. She grabbed a quiver of arrows from the pile, securing them on her back with the bow, climbed down out of her vantage point and jumped up onto the younger Jasban, who had moved and was waiting for her at the base of the burnt-out tree.

Sarah stood her ground and called out to her friends. "I had hoped that lot would have killed off our enemies but they still keep coming, this is it everyone. This is where we live or die!"

John shook his head. "This was supposed to be a holiday for me and an exciting time. Not a do or die moment!"

Rachel smiled weakly at John. "Work with what you have John, not with what you think that you should have, you never know, it might still just be a weird holiday? Whatever happens next John, my sister, Kate and I will do our best to protect you from the weirdness that is this place. We are all in this together now."

John noticed Rachel for the first time properly. "You are Sarah's sister, hey! You are one tough kid Rachel, thanks for that. I needed to hear it, you know how to make a kid feel welcome and you are a demon with a bow, just saying!"

Rachel almost blushed. No older boys had ever said anything like that to her, never paid her a compliment at all, now she came to think of it. She looked away towards Sarah and said to John. "No problem, just stick with Sarah. This is her place."

Sarah noticed the exchange, at any other time she might have smiled at it but right now everything was too intense. They may all be about to die. She drew two swords from her back pack then turned to the Horde. "If we are going to die at least let's take down as many of these nasties as we can. Maybe then the people we leave behind have a chance to finish them off."

Everyone except Dargal looked down into the ravine and raised their weapons. Kate stood and looked at Sarah. "Are you absolutely sure, no other tricks? No other traps?" Dargal had watched Kate and backed off from everyone else then melted away into the trees muttering Dwarvian curses and oaths under his breath.

Sarah could barely turn her face from the monsters coming towards her. "I'm absolutely sure, we have nothing left." Something in Kates voice sounded wrong, very wrong, she looked at John who was just staring at Kate, his eyes wide in surprise. As she turned her eyes to Kates she stepped back as the shock hit her!

Kates eyes were entirely black and she was smiling. While everything around them was dark and full of death! Her voice was silky smooth and she purred out gleefully. "I am so very glad to hear that 'Sarah the Adventurer'; I have waited so long to have you defenceless."

Sarah went to raise up her swords but Kate was too fast. Sarah found herself unable to move, frozen mid strike she gasped out. "Esmeralda!"

The Esmeralda grinned through Kate's face. "Yes Sarah, I am so hungry for your pain; it has been such a long time for me, so boring hiding in this woman's mind. Time to feast I think, who shall we start with, perhaps the boy?"

John watched not just in fear but also in fascination. He had only just met this woman, but this was not the woman he met. This was one of them, this woman had one of Them in her head and he knew what that felt like!

The Esmeralda threw her arm out and he was lifted high into the air as if he had been hit by a bus. John landed hard against a tree then fell groaning to the floor. Kate breathed in deeply and savoured the moment, breathing in the pain that emanated from him as he rolled on the ground groaning.

Rachel thought out in a panic to John. 'I have seen this Witch before, she got into my head but I escaped her. Robin helped me escape her.' Rachel still couldn't believe her eyes but slowly raised her bow and knocked an arrow hoping that 'The Esmeralda' hadn't noticed her yet. Just as she released the arrow The Esmeralda twisted her wrist and the arrow flew straight at Sarah embedding itself into her shoulder with the flint arrowhead sticking out of her back. Rachel gasped in horror at what she had just done to her own sister.

Sarah screamed out in pain, The Esmeralda stepped in close and took another deep breath, breathing in the pain then turned to Rachel. "And now for the little sister who betrayed me. Ahhhh, how much fun I am having!"

Rachel was shocked to the core and shouted out. "NO!"

The Jasban thought out. 'Hurt the girl Witch and I shall kill you where you stand'

The Esmeralda laughed and thought back to him. 'Oh, tiny monster, you know that you and your little brother were never a match for one like me.' She looked over to one of the fallen boulders, as she lifted her arm the boulder rose into the air. Sweeping her arm towards the Jasban, the boulder flew through the air and smashed into the side of him knocking him off his feet and sending Rachel tumbling to the ground.

The other Jasban and Brian both went to leap at her but again she raised her hands and they found themselves frozen to the spot as she said out loud. "Oh, come on everyone, I know I said I was hungry but this is too easy! I shall have to save torturing some of you for dessert." She walked slowly around the troupe of fallen and frozen friends.

Sarah shouted out through her pain. "Leave them alone Witch. They have done nothing to you!"

The Esmeralda laughed at Sarah. "Really Sarah? Have the Frow ever done you any harm? Of course not, but you still eat them don't you, they are still your food aren't they? Well your pain is my food and yours in particular tastes," she paused and sniffed the air around Sarah, "so sweet, so sweet like revenge!" She grabbed the arrow in Sarah's shoulder and twisted it slowly, cruelly around. Sarah grunted out in pain but still looked defiantly at the Witch.

Rachel managed to stand up and shout through her own tears. "Why? Why do you hate my sister so much?"

The Esmeralda spun round to Rachel. "You don't know? You don't know what Sarah the Adventurer did do you?" Then she turned back to Sarah and laughed. "Oh Sarah. What lies have you told them? Did you feel so bad about what you did that you made up stories? Did you not tell them about the Bucket, about your Bucket and what you did to it?"

Tears of pain filled Sarah's eyes and she stood unable to move or even slump down in despair. Rachel shouted out. "What is she talking about Sarah?"

Sarah looked daggers at the Witch through her tears and shouted back to Rachel. "I had no choice Rachel! Please believe me, I'm so sorry!"

The Esmeralda leaned in and stroked Sarah's face "Oh emotional pain, this is almost too sweet. Tell her Sarah, tell them all what you did. Sarah, let's call it therapy."

Sarah said nothing but looked at Rachel, then at Brian. Tears rolled down her face unchecked, after a long sad moment Sarah revealed her guilty secret. "I killed it. I melted it down so that this Witch couldn't have it, couldn't use it or me. I didn't know then that it lived, I didn't know that they are living things that stay with us through our lives, I killed mine and I cry every time I think about it. I killed my friend!" Tears streamed down her face, dripping onto the ground as her heart threatened to beat itself out of her chest.

The Esmeralda twisted the arrow in Sarah's shoulder again. "Yes, you did and you stopped me from growing, stopped me from going to your world to learn and feed for so many years. Such a spiteful murdering child you are, killing your own lifelong friend!"

Rachel felt a sudden vibration on her hip and looked down to see her Bucket glowing. She had forgotten it was even there. Everything about it now made sense. She felt a new warmth towards it, now that she knew it was alive. She understood too how desperate Sarah must have been.

Bruised as he was John looked down as his own Bucket vibrated. He was surprised to see it still strapped to his hip, his mind was racing as he remembered what it had felt like when his mind was taken over by one of the Alder. His thoughts were interrupted, he heard a familiar voice inside his head. 'Look up mate, I'm guessing you might need a 'mate' right now.'

John looked up and smiled. He had an idea and threw it back up into the air. 'Yes mate, I do need a 'mate'. Can you do this?' He thought out an image that he created in his head of the Griffin swooping down.

Robin responded. 'Yep, we can do that!'

Brian thought out to the group. 'Don't believe her Sarah, you did what you did for all the right reasons as a small child.' He looked The Esmeralda in the eye as he thought out. 'She is the evil one, she lives off causing pain, spreading fear and twisting truths. I told you before that you are not to blame, you must believe me!'

The Alder were nearly upon them. Their approach slowed as they heard the voice of the guardian in their hive mind. 'I am not dead. Wait upon my pleasure and I will instruct you.'

The hive mind was confused, it had its purpose, it was here to kill the 'Slayer'. Many of its number had died in the battle already. 'You were killed, we felt it, now we must have a new Guardian, a new Queen!'

The Esmeralda turned to the horde which now surrounded them. 'My body died yes, but I did not, the Slayer killed my body but I have evolved past a physical presence. I have evolved past you all, I am stronger than you and I am no longer content to simply be the Guardian to Monsters!'

The swarm moved threateningly around them all creeping up the gorge and moving among the trees, then repeated a long-held thought 'The Slayer must die. Then we shall have a new Guardian from one of us.'

The Esmeralda stopped and looked around at the tentacled monsters with disgust and pity. 'I almost feel sorry for you. I have been in so many minds over these hundreds of years whilst you slept in those caves, I have outgrown you beasts who feed from the pain of cave bears and worms and lurk underground. I have become all powerful, I have evolved past feeding off of the elemental.' She shouted into everyone's minds. 'I am 'The Esmeralda' I am closer to being a God than a mortal, I am all and everything and you will obey me!'

She raised her arms slowly, lifting the entire horde of utterly surprised monsters into the air a few feet and then dropped them back to the ground. As they regained their footing they scuttled backwards away from her, like petrified dogs who had been beaten by their master.

She walked slowly around in triumph. "Soon I shall feed on your pain Sarah and after I have had my fill…." She said turning to John and Rachel, "I will use one of your portals to take me back to your world. This time I shall grow even stronger!" Spreading her arms wide she twirled around in the joy of her absolute victory.

The voices of the swarm filled her head. 'The Slayer is ours, we must kill the slayer!'

The Esmeralda hung Kates head down in mock despair and irritation. 'Are you such stupid creatures, such drones. I shouldn't have expected so much from you should I. The Slayer is mine to feed from. You can have the rest of the creatures here. She did not slay me you fools, she freed me from you, that body died but I evolved, I am 'The Esmeralda', there is only one of me, I am unique!'

The voice from the Alder came in unison into everyone's minds. 'You are one of us no more.'

The Esmeralda thought back. 'At last you get it! No, I am not one of you, I am more than all of you now!' Then she turned back to Sarah ignoring the Alder surrounding them and stroked Sarah's tear drenched face. "You are a murderer of your own living portal. You lied to your friends. Worst of all you have betrayed your sister by pretending to be her friend when all along you knew you were not worthy of her love."

Sarah looked back at the Witch and nearly broke altogether. "I didn't mean to hurt anything or anyone, I didn't..."

Brian thought out to Sarah. 'Don't listen to her Sarah, she speaks the truth but twists it, she is deluded and mad. You only did what you did to stop her evil from spreading. You were young but I remember, the Minotaur and Kobalos both know the truth, believe me, the bucket you melted down wasn't your bucket. Kobalos swapped it when he discovered what you were going to do!'

The Esmeralda turned to the trapped Unicorn and spoke sharply and angrily. "Really Brian, really? They should believe you over me? I am ancient, wise and I have only spoken the truth have I not? Why should anyone believe you?"

Brian whinnied as the huge Griffin swooped down out of the air with Robin clinging onto its neck. It grabbed The Esmeralda in its claws lifting her bodily off of the ground, trapping her arms by her sides as she screamed out in surprise, rage and frustration. 'Let me loose Griffin, I can make you suffer as much as anyone!'

The Griffin thought down to the Witch. 'We have been aware of you for a long time Queen of the Alder. You are arrogant and your threats do not concern us, your magic does not affect us. We are Kobaloi, we are Griffin!'

Robin shouted down from atop the massive and beautifully proud creature flying majestically through the air.

"Sarah, John reckons that we have to body shock 'The Witch' out of Kate. If we manage it I'll be back I promise! What's that sticking out of your shoulder?'

Brian shouted his thought to answer The Esmeralda. "Because I am a Unicorn Witch, pure of heart, as honest and deep as a winter frost and I never lie!' Then he turned his thoughts to Sarah. 'Sarah, I know that you are good to the core, I cannot give my breath to anyone not pure of heart, it is not physically possible. The Minotaur holds your bucket still. It is time to believe in yourself. It is time to fight!'

Sarah started to move, slowly she began to push through the inertia that the Witch had put upon her, she managed to lower her swords and step forward. "We can move, we can push past her magic! Don't worry about me Robin, just take the Witch as far away from us as possible.'

John thought directly up to Kate as the Griffin took her body in flight away from them all. 'Kate, I know you are still in there. You have to kick that bitch out of your head somehow, I know that you are still in there, can you hear me? I had one in my head and I know that you can beat it.'

Kate could hear him, yet she was in a strange place inside her own head. She felt the physical pain of being held in the claws of a Griffin but could only see in her mind's eye the wall of darkness that was trapping her. She found the strength from within to whisper out. 'I am still here, I am so comfortable, so warm and cosy but my throat hurts'. All she could see in her mind's eye though was a cloud of darkness and comfort.

John was broken and bruised, yet had just enough strength to think out to her. 'When I was infected by one of these 'things' Clara slapped me just hard enough to knock it out my head without killing me. Robin is going to find a way to body shock you without killing you, hopefully?' And then thought out to Robin. 'Work with what you have kid, eh?'

Robin thought out a windswept shout from the back of the Griffin. 'Okay, I'll think of something.' The Griffin wheeled away down towards the Creek, away from the group who were now surrounded by a swarm of angry and confused Alder. The Esmeralda screamed her rage at Robin from the claws of the Griffin.

Brian and the Jasban started to move, slowly at first but heeding Sarah's words they pushed harder and began to release themselves from the grip of the Witch.

The Alder saw movement and just like a cat sensing the vulnerability of injured prey, put its confusion away and shouted into everyone's minds. 'We have come for the Slayer and she will die now, the Guardian is gone, we shall find a new Guardian!' The group felt the Alder tense up ready to attack.

This was it! Even though the Witch was not a direct threat at the moment, they still faced the Monsters who were moving slowly towards them, they could sense the inevitability of their own deaths stalking them.

One of the Alder leapt onto the back of the fallen Jasban and began flailing his tentacles to slice pieces out of the already stricken beast. The Jasban squealed in pain. It was a sound that no-one had ever heard before. His brother strained against the inertia he was set in but was moving too slowly to stop the creatures attack.

They were still moving too slowly from the grip of the Witch to help. They thought out in frustration and support for him to hold fast. A sound that they all knew rang in their ears. It was the blood curdling roar of the Minotaur!

Sarah turned slowly. She was very surprised to see that, way down the Ravine, the Minotaur was grabbing at the Alder. They were almost equal his size yet lacked both his muscle and his fury. Alongside him was a smartly suited man (who looked very out of place) wearing dark glasses, he was swinging two swords back and forth, despatching Alder's heads and tentacles from their bodies like that was what he had been trained to do all of his life!

Even though this was a plus for them, still the Alder were too many, the group were surrounded with one still torturing the Jasban. Rachel was unaffected by the inertia but was physically exhausted from firing arrows. She summoned up the strength from somewhere deep within to grab the bow from her back. Although her arm ached in pain she still managed to knock and loose one last arrow at the creature that was torturing the Jasban. The arrow missed its target and skipped along the ground. Rachel looked to Sarah with a genuine thought of, 'Sorry sis, I'm done in!' With that she slumped down to the ground, totally wiped out.

It only took seconds for an Alder to jump over, standing above Rachel it swept its long tentacles to one side, lifting her from the ground and body slammed her against the very tree that had been her refuge. Rachel slid unconscious to the ground.

The Monster stood, poised ready to strike. It turned to Sarah as it thought out slowly with black eyes gleaming in triumph. 'You're next Slayer, YOU are next!' Its tentacles swirled around just as something moved out from the undergrowth right next to it. Dargal leapt out from his hiding place swirling his small but very effective sword around and sliced three tentacles from the creature before it knew what was happening.

The Alder screamed out in pain, turned on Dargal, kicking out at him with powerful limbs and sending the poor Dwarf tumbling back down the Ravine.

Sarah called down to the Minotaur. "I heard you, help us old friend we are losing. I am so sorry for killing my portal!" Sarah was an emotional wreck right now.

The Minotaur roared out again. "What are you talking about Sarah? I still have your portal, I have been nursing it all these years past. Kobalos swapped your portal many years ago to save it from the Witch. He is always one step ahead, the little cockroach!"

Sarah gasped as a thousand emotions ran through her body and brain. Guilt melted from her like an ice cube against a blow torch, now she began to understand her journey! The Witch really had tricked her all these years, Brian was right, she wasn't to blame after all. Now she really believed!

The Minotaur's thoughts burst into her mind again. 'We are trying to crush these evil things Sarah but there are too many of them!' Sure enough the Alder were beginning to pull down the Minotaur, despite the Agent killing many of them as efficiently as he could, in an effort to defend his superior and himself.

The Minotaur's voice began to fade. 'Sorry Sarah, this may be the last time I see you. These creatures are too strong and are killing me. I never thought I would see my own death?' She could almost feel the pain that the monsters were inflicting upon him.

Sarah felt the earth shake as the Minotaur fell to his knees. Summoning all the strength she could muster in her mind and body, she managed to break free of the final grip of the Witch. Rachel stepped forwards, able now to move freely she shouted out to the Monster holding Rachel. "Stop! Take me! Stop them from hurting the Minotaur! I won't fight you anymore. Don't hurt her, please!" Her voice was desperate and pleading. "Kill me, it's me you want. You will be the new Queen and Guardian. I promise that I won't cause you any trouble but leave her alone, please, please don't hurt the Minotaur, don't hurt my little sister!" Tears of despair fell from her eyes.

The other Alder stopped approaching and waited as the monster above Rachel slowly moved its tentacles around and down. They slipped slowly under Rachel's inert form then lifted her into the air. 'I don't need your 'Permission' to feed human.' Sarah watched in horror as it raised one of its tentacles up to strike Rachel.

The Jasban squealed out in pain as its torturer sliced out another chunk of flesh with its whip like tentacles.

Sarah knew in that moment that all her sins had come to punish her at once. She had put her little sister in danger, put them all in danger and now they would die and it was all because of her!

Then a new voice sounded in everyone's mind. It was coming from somewhere up the Ravine, a familiar voice and a scolding voice at that! 'Sarah Jameson! I knew that if there was trouble around that you would be at the heart of it!'

Sarah's mind summersaulted in surprise and disbelief. 'Mrs Mole?'

CHAPTER EIGHTEEN

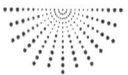

Robin searched his mind. 'Hmmmm, body shock?' The Griffin wheeled round and down into the creek with its beautiful living eco-system of colourful flowers, insect clouds and waterfalls. Everything seemed really crazy, it was like being caught up in a tornado with everything outside utterly calm and still.

The Witch scre*amed* her thoughts into his mind as they sailed through the skies. 'How dare you touch me boy! Tell this thing to let me go or I shall make you suffer. I shall render your skin from your body, crush your bones within you, I shall make every nerve ending in your body scream in pain and then I shall…'

Robin listened knowing that if or when the Griffin let loose its grip on the Witch that she could bring those horrors upon him. He looked out below for whatever could be a 'Body shock'? He couldn't ask the Griffin to just drop The

Witch against the rocks because that would kill her host's body which was Kate.

He searched his surroundings, looking down into the centre of the creek he saw the river, cold and furious as it was, it held the answer. Water! Witches hate water he thought. From somewhere deep in his mind he remembered from fairy-tales and stories, witches hate water.

He shuffled his way forwards and as the witch screamed '….and then I shall tear your body apart slowly and I…' Robin shouted out into the mind of Kobalos and the Kobaloi that constituted the Griffin. 'Drop her now, drop her into the water!' The Griffin did just that, releasing his claws as it soared over the river.

Kates body with its Witch occupied mind fell screaming in surprise through the air, down towards the raging river at the centre of the creek. Before even a hair on her head got wet its descent stopped abruptly, just a couple of metres from the rivers surface, then began to rise slowly into the air.

The Esmeralda screeched a thought out to Robin as she smiled smugly up at him. 'You thwarted me once before boy, you took your sister from me but now I am more powerful, I have learned from you!' Kate's body turned, she lay like an upside-down sky diver looking up at him in the air and threw her arms wide. 'My turn now boy, now you will die!'

Robin knew he had only a second to act, so he did something idiotic, totally stupid and impulsive, just like his Dad would have done if he were here. He slid down off the Griffin's neck and dropped into the empty air below him hurtling down directly towards the floating Witch!

She in turn looked up in utter surprise that any being could be so stupid as to fling itself into the air from such a height to fall to his own inevitable death. Her eyes widened as she suddenly realised that he was hurtling down from the back of the Griffin directly at her and would hit her in a matter of seconds!

Robin looked downwards in total fear but caught the Witches eye, he grinned and shouted out. "If I am going to die Witch then I am taking you with me. I will stop you from hurting my Sarah anymore!" Then spread his arms out wide to catch her as he fell.

Their bodies collided mid-air in a body slam before The Witch had a chance to repel him with her magic. Kate's breath was knocked out of her lungs, as they hit he embraced her, trapping her arms by her sides. The force of the impact dragged her out of the mid-air stasis, sending them both plummeting down towards the freezing waters of the creek below them.

Robin was now face to face with the Witch, which was weird. He seized his opportunity to vent his anger as they careered towards the icy waters. "I thought Sarah had killed you, you should be dead but you came back to hurt her, that ain't going to happen witch!" he shouted.

Her black eyes bore into his glowing blue eyes. "I am immortal stupid boy, I cannot die! You might kill this body but I shall live forever!"

They hit the water with a huge splash and sank below the surface. The shock from the cold was intense. Robin instinctively let go of his captive and started swimming back up to the light of the day above.

Kate immediately came back to herself and swam up following Robin. The Witch had indeed been knocked out of her mind and Kate could feel it trying to take back control. Things were different this time, Kate knew what the Witch was and where she really was.

As she broke the surface she gasped in air deeply and swam to the river bank.

Robin and Kate reached the shore about the same time, they both flopped down onto the grass out of shock and exhaustion. Robin rolled over and looked at Kate lying on the shore next to him. She turned her head towards him and said the weirdest thing. "Strangle me Robin. Do it now Robin or she'll be back in my head in seconds and no one will be safe, strangle me now!"

Robin dragged himself onto his knees, crawled over to Kate and watched in frustration as her eyes began to fill with the blackness of The Witch. He heard Kate say in desperation. "It's in my throat, get it out!"

He put his hands around Kate's throat and hesitated for a moment. The Witch's silky voice came from within Kate again. "Why would you kill this woman Robin, I have never killed anything, caused them pain to feed, yes, but I don't kill. Are you really capable of murder boy?"

Robin's eyes narrowed as he noticed it! He saw the

movement in Kate's neck, like something was pushing outwards. He made his resolve there and then, he pressed his thumbs down hard and then even harder. As he did so he heard The Witch in his head pleading for Kate's life. 'Don't kill her Robin, you killed a Dragon and it hurt you didn't it? Just imagine what it would be like to kill a human.'

Robin looked into the black eyes of The Witch and shouted out loud. "If Kate dies and that kills you, I don't think she would care, so die now Witch!" He continued pressing his thumbs hard into Kate's throat but there was a resistance. He pushed as hard as he could, he felt something wriggle under his thumbs, he kept pushing and pressing with all his might. Kate's mouth started to open and he saw it.

Looking like the head of a snake something tried to escape from the pressure of his thumbs. His eyes widened in horror at what he was seeing as it began to emerge. It was as black as the Witches eyes but purple and bulbous as well, it had eyes but they were closed against the light of the day. Without thinking Robin quickly grabbed the head, pulled it hard and its whole long lumpy, slimy body slid out from Kate's throat.

As it left her body, she lifted her head and retched more mucus out from the pit of her stomach, rolled herself over and tried to drag herself to her knees.

Robin had a tight grip on the parasite but within seconds its tail wrapped itself around his neck. It started to squeeze hard, just like a boa constrictor does around its prey. He heard the Witches voice scream furiously into his mind. 'You will be the first thing I have ever actually killed boy and I really didn't want to hurt you Robin!'

Robin choked in surprise, slipping his free hand into his pocket he pulled out Sarah's necklace. In one swift motion he squeezed the little silver ball hard in the palm of his hand and shoved it into the open mouth of the creature. He followed the path of the Witches thoughts back into its head. 'I don't know what you really are but this should shut you up once and for all!'

The creature's eyes opened briefly, they looked pitiful for a brief second as she thought back. 'You can kill this body Robin, like you killed the Dragon I was in, but before I die please know this. It was you I was seeking all this time, not Sarah, you are beautiful and can set me free!' It's grip around Robins neck tightened briefly, he could feel the creatures lies, then the long slimy body convulsed and let go of him.

The look was so pitiful that Robin almost felt sorry for it, then it hissed at him, the ball in its mouth exploded in a light that even Robin couldn't bear to look at. A water bubble grew and grew in the Esmeralda, its body swelled but was unable to contain the huge volume of water, suddenly it reached its limit and exploded in his hand like an enormous water balloon (but way messier).

He knelt for a moment holding the sagging fleshy skin and staring at the mess that covered him. The sudden acrid stench was repulsive.

He fell back onto the shore of the river, exhausted and stunned, his mind and body buzzing. He felt Kate's hand slip into his as she lay next to him also feeling wiped out and exhausted. "Thank you, Robin," she slowly gasped out. "Thank you!" Kate rolled her head round on the shore to look him in the eye. "You are my saviour!" Then with a deep slow breath said. "Is it over now, is she really dead?"

The pair lay looking up at the two suns, feeling the warmth of its rays on their skin, breathing heavily and listening to the water rush by for a few calming, exhausted moments. Robin looked back at her. "Yes Kate, it is dead, totally!"

Kate smiled at Robin. "I feel like I've just been through a very long, slow car crash. I am utterly confused and exhausted, thank you Robin McRacker. Oh! And thank you for not killing me. Just one more thing though."

Robin looked at her "What?"

Kate smiled. "We reeeeeally stink!"

Robin smiled back. "God, yes we do!" he laughed a bit madly. "God yes we really do!

A panic sprang into Robins mind as he shouted out. "Sarah!" Just then the shadow of the most amazing creature that they would ever see or understand swooped down and landed on the riverbank right next to them.

The Griffin crouched and talked into their minds. 'This is not over; the Alder are still swarming. Your friends may die, these creatures must be stopped, we see that now. Climb up quickly.'

CHAPTER NINETEEN

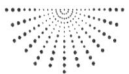

Mrs Mole stood atop a boulder with a longbow stretched and ready to let loose her arrow. The hair tied up in a high pony tail was a testament to her 'meaning business'. This was definitely not the Mrs Mole that Sarah left here some years ago who had been an uptight, very formal Guides leader, somewhat conservative and an insecurely 'stressed-out' middle-aged lady of repute. Mrs Mole had travelled and was clearly a very different person now. To Sarah she looked 'awesome!'

Standing on that boulder now was a female warrior, dressed in Frow leather hide, sword tucked into a scabbard on her back and a quiver of arrows strapped to her belt. She looked primed and ready to inflict serious damage on anything that stood in her way!

Sarah reached up to the painful arrow in her shoulder, then looked over in amazement at the woman who used to be her Guide leader, at least for a short while, in the human world.

Mrs Mole then loosed the arrow, it flew swiftly through the air and straight through the head of the Alder creature that had been holding Rachel. The Alder's eyes widened in disbelief as it dropped slowly to the ground, relaxing its hand it released Rachel from its grip.

At that moment a boulder hurtled past Mrs Mole down through the Ravine, unfurled herself just in time to catch Rachels unconscious body. She trilled in glee at catching this little girl she knew so well and looked at the Alder who fell lifeless to the ground before her, still with a shocked look on its face.

Sarah gasped. "Clara Frab! Is she alive? Is she okay?"

Clara Frab ran her hands over Rachel and looked at Sarah. Her Kaleidoscopic eyes crinkled as she though back. 'Rachel child good'.

Sarah looked at Mrs Mole in utter incredulity as another voice came into her head, it was one which filled her heart with a joy that made the pain of the arrow in her shoulder almost disappear. She heard White Tiger's deep voice croon into her mind. 'Little sister, Sarah two legs, we found my family and it looks like the Frab found us just in time for you!'

Sarah's heart nearly broke with the joy of hearing that voice in her head, the voice of her 'little brother'. She shook her head in wonder as over a hundred other White Tigers, almost as huge as her childhood friend, came racing down to meet the Alder. 'I am so glad to see you little brother and...' she hesitated to find the words, '...and this is your family?'

The others around Sarah also looked out in awe at the oncoming streak of White Tigers that were headed directly for the rest of the Alder. White Tiger himself sauntered into view. 'My family are hungry Sarah, is it against the rules to eat these creatures?'

Sarah smiled and ran towards him free of the Witches spell. 'Let them eat their fill White whiskers but only the monsters!' Even with the arrow sticking through her right shoulder and out the other side she threw her left arm up and hugged the best friend that she had ever had. She sent him a private thought as tears fell from her eyes. 'I have missed you so much little brother, thank you, thank you so much for saving my sister.'

White Tiger lay down in front of her so that they were at the same height and purred out. 'I am glad to see you too big sister.' Turning his head to the others he thought out. 'Kill only the ugly looking ones that look like this' and he sent out an image of the Alder into the heads of every Tiger in the ravine. 'Lill them all and take your fill of them!'

The Alder turned to run from the onslaught but were too late as the Tigers flowed around the troupe and leapt onto the backs of Sarah's enemies. With huge claws gripping into flesh and tearing the monsters apart. The sound of the Alder screaming as one after another died in agony was a sound that Sarah was glad Rachel would not remember.

Sarah heard the Minotaur shout out his thanks in a growl

to the new allies. The Agent and he continued their struggle to kill as many of these parasites as they could but now they had the advantage of numbers.

The Agent looked out in confusion as the Tigers appeared, ripping the Alder apart as they came. He stood still, lowered his weapons and said to the Minotaur. "I believe that we have done our part and should step back now?"

The Minotaur swirled around looking for new enemies but finding none heeded the Human's words. "You are right, strange human, we must let nature take its course!"

Away up the Ravine, beyond the carnage that the Minotaur and Agent had just witnessed, Brian whinnied. An ancient part of him instinctively made him trot to the safety of the Jasban, just as Dargal re-appeared, limping and saying as he looked over his shoulder at the fleeing Alder. "Those tigers are stealing all of my fun! I was just getting into my stride."

The younger Jasban jumped into the air, ran in a circle and despite the pain, drooled out his joy at seeing their old and yet very dangerous friend Dargal.

The older Jasban barked out his thoughts to White Tiger even as he lay in a painful heap on the ground. 'You missed all the fun Fluffy, you wouldn't believe what has been going on here. I have been to the Human's world. That is one strange place, I never want to go back there again!'

White Tiger did the closest equivalent of smiling that he could and thought out to both Jasban. 'We shall have time to tell our stories' but now let's finish this.'

With that White Tiger, the younger Jasban and Brian turned to join White Tiger's new family, running towards the last of the Alder.

Sarah fell to her knees in pain as John and Dargal rushed over to her side. "You okay kid? You look wiped out?"

Sarah looked at them both. "I'm fine but Rachel, check Rachel for me, make sure she's okay!"

John rushed over to Sarah's little sister who Clara was holding and stroking tenderly, he leaned down. "She's breathing!"

Mrs Mole had jumped down from the boulder. She swung round a bag from her back as she reached Sarah and was immediately full of concern, looking at the arrow in her right shoulder. "Well Sarah, here you are in a pickle again! Let's see, I think that you know what I have to do here don't you? I learned a lot about you from White Tiger on our travels, we shall have time to talk about that but for now…" and here she drew a small piece of wood from her back pack along with a small pot. She gave Sarah the piece of wood and said. "…bite down on this when it hurts. When we are done, I shall take a look at Rachel."

Sarah looked at Mrs Mole with new understanding, knowing that she had changed from being a 'Guide Leader' to being a friend of White Tiger and an adventurer, just like her.

She took the wood and put it in her mouth as Mrs Mole smeared a cold gel along the sides of the arrow shaft. Sarah braced herself for the pain, looked Mrs Mole in the eye and nodded.

Mrs Mole saw Sarah's nod. In one swift move she broke the shaft of the arrow at the front, drew the rest of it straight through Sarah's shoulder and out the back of her. Sarah bit down hard, grimaced and grunted at the severe pain.

Within seconds Mrs Mole covered both sides of Sarah's wounds in a healing gel and a moss plaster, then reached back down into her bag, pulled out what looked like a pair of furry spiders that crawled hungrily around her hand and put one each side of Sarah's shoulder. "These little wonders will suck any poison out and help your shoulder heal young Sarah. You'll be fine now, well, soon anyway. Right then, let's take a look at my star Brownie Rachel."

Mrs Mole walked over to an unconscious Rachel. She put up her hand with fingers spread wide to Clara who was kneeling protectively over Rachel. As their fingers touched Clara smiled, Mrs Mole smiled back and thought out to Clara. 'Moley back Clara and Moley see's that Clara really is individual!'

Clara trilled out in pure joy and love for her friend. Mrs Mole took Rachel's hand feeling her pulse, then bent down and listened to her breathing. She ran her hands firmly but with care up and down checking for breaks or fractures. "No more than exhaustion and bruises I think, nothing broken Clara Frab. She will be fine with rest, you all look like you need rest and nourishment."

She lifted Rachel up into a sitting position and rubbed her

back tenderly as Rachel began to wake. Groggily through bleary eyes simply asked "Sarah?"

Sarah was by her side in seconds, the relief of hearing her little sisters voice was clear to everyone. "I'm here Sis, it's okay, we're safe, it's over."

Rachel's voice was weak but she asked the question that Sarah had been dreading. "Can we go home now sis?"

Sarah put her good arm around her sister, looked up at John, Dargal and Moley, at the Minotaur striding towards her with the strange man in his suit by his side. "Soon Rach, maybe soon!" Her little sister smiled and then fell back into a deep sleep.

Mrs Mole looked around at everyone. "I think it time for some food and sleep for most of you. Don't you agree Sarah?"

Sarah looked back at Mrs Mole still in some awe and reverted back to being in a village hall trying to please her Guides leader a bit. "Um, yes, back up to my home cave then, we have fruit and cured Frow meat still. Well if it's still edible that is. Jasban will you help me take Rachel?"

The older Jasban had managed to stand despite his wounds and purred. 'She is a little sister to me now Sarah, of course I will.' With that he knelt down by his small ward and thought out to Sarah. 'Rachel is awesome for a human female!'

Mrs Mole though wasn't finished. "Now then." and she turned to Clara directly. "You and I have some catching up to do, because Clara Frab you are the same and yet as separate a

Frab as I have ever seen and we both have stories to share. I gave you your name Clara, but you seem to have been on your own journey it seems and I would like to hear about that. Clara Frab, I am so very proud of you."

Mrs Mole stood up as Clara also stood up and leaned down to Moley, Clara having grown not just in spirit and personality but also in size, they embraced as their hearts beat at the same pace.

Clara Frab smiled broadly. 'Moley gave Frab name but Clara Frab got lost in Human world and Frab felt alone. 'Idiot boy' found Frab and made Frab feel like Clara Frab.' Then her eyes widened. 'Idiot boy, Clara forget to save idiot boy, Clara mean Robin, not idiot boy anymore!'

John heard her and said. "If you mean Robin then I think that he's okay Clara, I think he will be here soon, I hope!"

Clara smiled at John and said out loud. "Clara glad Clara not kill John. Clara glad Moley come to help."

Mrs Mole looked at Clara in some surprise. "You can speak Clara Frab, you are the first Frab that I have ever heard actually speak out loud!"

Clara smiled. "Clara learn from Robin and John Kid. Robin kind to Clara always, Clara listen, Clara practice, Clara learn."

Brian trotted back close enough for Sarah to hear him in her mind. 'Sarah, the Alder are no more. I can feel that the Witch is truly dead. For the first time in your life in this world 'Sarah the Adventurer' you are free of them, all of them. For the first time since you came here as a child you now have no enemies, well maybe the Cratalorg but they hate everyone.'

He trotted over to her and stood by her side. 'You are free to go back to your world, or to stay in this one. This might be your third and final choice though, so take your time making your decision. But know this, you are free in both worlds now and you have our everlasting gratitude'.

Sarah looked down at her little sister with her heart full of love. "I have made my choice Brian, now that White Tiger has found his family, I think it is time that I went home to mine."

The noise of the final destruction of the Alder had ended and the plethora of White Tigers were now feasting on their prey. It was not a sound anyone really wanted to hear and yet it was a sound that everyone there was glad, really glad to hear. The ravine fell quiet bar some unpleasant crunching of bones, tearing of flesh and slurping noises, thankfully they were some way off.

Sarah looked at Brian with uncertainty, then over at Rachel who was lying down on the grassy bank. "I think I know where I belong now. Where's Robin? Is he alive?"

Just as she finished talking Robin's voice came in to her mind, her heart began to pound in an unusual way as she caught sight of the immense form of the Griffin. It circled around and down from high above like a plane coming into land. 'Looks like it's over Sarah. I killed the witch properly this time; Can you believe that! And Kate is, well, Kate again. The Witch was a parasite that was in Kates throat but I got it out and killed it with that ball you gave me. I think we won, I think that it's over and there is something else that I need to tell you.' His thoughts came out in a rush that he couldn't stop, he had something really important to tell her.

Sarah heard his voice in her mind, her heart felt like it was beating in her mouth, he was safe and he had killed the Witch, he was properly awesome! Oddly Mrs Mole's scolding words came back to her. "The leaf does not fall far from the tree!" She pondered her de-facto father Jack and realised that Robin was just as nuts as his dad was. She felt glad that the leaf did not fall far from the tree.

As the Griffin landed in the Ravine right next to Sarah, Kate slid down off of its neck and walked over unsteadily. "I am so sorry Sarah, the Witch was a creature that infested me, I am so sorry that she used me to get to you, please believe me that if I had known what it was I…"

Sarah cut her off. "Kate, you were and are one of the best and most wonderful humans that I have ever known. You protected me and mine, became my friend despite unknowingly hosting my enemy, you don't have to be sorry. If the Witch is dead then we can both be glad, she was the enemy of us both." She stepped forward and gave Kate a one-armed hug. Her right arm was still very sore but felt a lot better now there wasn't an arrow sticking through it.

Kate smiled and let a tear drop as her emotions, her true emotions welled up inside. Standing back from Sarah she whispered for her ears only. "You are the most amazing girl I have ever known!" Sarah smiled a thank you and turned to look at the reason why her heart was beating in a weird way.

Robin stood waiting next to the Griffin, stroking its fur and feathers as Sarah walked towards him. "I'm pretty sure that the Witch is properly dead now Sarah. I have got to say this now, it's something that I have wanted to say for some time but I'm not sure quite how to say it!"

Sarah stood and waited hopefully and expectantly looking into Robin's eyes. "Yes?"

Robin became the nervous kid that had stood at the gate to her house when Mrs Jameson had challenged him. "Well, I wanted to say that I, um, well the reason that… I sort of…"

Sarah put Robin out of his awkward misery, wrapped her good arm around him and slowly kissed him full on. His eyes widened in utter surprise and relief. She drew back slightly and said whilst looking lovingly into his eyes. "Don't worry Robin, I know and I feel the same way about you, you are awesome!"

Everyone else in the Ravine looked away in slight awkwardness for a brief second before looking back to smile their approval!

John called over to Robin. "Hey kid, looks like you didn't die then! Glad you made it, does this mean we can go home now or will you be picking a fight with something else here?"

Robin smiled at John. "I'm done with fighting mate and thanks John, I don't think I would be here if it weren't for you. I think it's definitely time to go home." Robin pulled away from Sarah's embrace and asked in some panic. "Rach! Is Rachel okay? Where is she? Is she here?"

Sarah smiled and looked to Clara. "Yes Robin, she's over there with Clara Frab and Mrs Mole."

Robin looked around and saw Clara holding Rachel close to her as Rachel slept. "Mrs Mole! You look very different to how I remember you!"

Mrs Mole laughed. "Well I certainly feel different Robin McRacker but now is not about me is it? We need to get Rachel to somewhere she can rest and frankly the rest of you could do with food, a rest and a good wash, especially you young McRacker, what have you been rolling in?"

Kate answered for Robin whilst stepping to his side. "Glory, he has been rolling in glory. He just saved my life and possibly everyone else's here!" Then she addressed Mrs Mole. "I'm Kate Bradworth and you are?"

Mrs Mole smiled warmly at this woman who was clearly close to Sarah. "Well I used to be Mrs Mole but these days most creatures here just call me Moley. I think that we all have some stories to share, don't we?"

Then Moley looked at Sarah. "Sarah, White Tiger has told me so much about you that I was unaware of. I am sorry that I was so harsh on you when you were in the Guides!"

Sarah smiled. "No worries Moley, I'm looking forward to hearing how you tamed my little brother though!" Looking to Clara she asked. "Can you carry Rach up to my cave Clara, if you sit on the Jasban's back? It's not far up the ravine and I need to know that she is okay, I need to make sure that my little sister is really okay?"

Clara trilled and spoke out loud. "Clara Frab feel like Clara Frab have new family and Clara Frab always help family."

Robin walked over to Clara and stood in front of her. "You are an incredible friend Clara, thank you for being there for me and us all."

Clara trilled again. "Robin boy save Clara, Clara not save Robin boy but help save Robin boys friends. Is that ok Robin boy?"

Robin smiled back at her. "That is more than okay Clara Frab, you have been so brave, you will always be my friend. Clara Frab did just fine."

Clara stretched down and drew Robin to her for a hug. 'Clara thank Robin for making Clara, Clara.' Robin smiled and hugged her back.

White Tiger sauntered back into view with a sea of tigers following behind. 'No more creatures to kill Sarah but it felt good to finish them off. You are safe now.'

Sarah looked at White Tiger and the family he had found since she last saw him. 'White Tiger, you know that I have always loved you but…'

White Tiger purred as he finished off her sentence. 'But you have to go to your home, to your family and that is as it should be. I shall always remember you as my big sister 'Sarah the Adventurer.'

Sarah hugged White Tiger with her good arm. 'You will

always be my little brother 'White Whiskers' and I shall always love you.'

Mrs Mole looked at Rachel then called to Sarah. "Time to go Sarah."

Sarah let go of White Tiger looked up and down the Ravine and nodded. She placed her good hand in Robins and the group turned to walk up the ravine towards her cave. "You know you don't look much like Jack but you are definitely as crazy as he is!"

Robin looked surprised at her and then smiled to himself then back at her "I'll take that Sarah the Adventurer, I'll take that!"

CHAPTER TWENTY

Mr and Mrs Jameson were searching the remains of their house for anything that could be salvaged from the carnage that the Dragons had wreaked. The McRacker's were doing the same next door but one. Most of the houses down the street had been fairly badly decimated and other people were returning to save what they could from their own properties. They were being helped by soldiers, workmen and structural engineers who were ensuring that the houses were actually safe to enter.

The house between the McRacker's and the Jameson's though was the only house that was entirely untouched, it was the empty property where Rachel had first heard the strange noises coming from and that had a green glow coming from it. The house where this had all begun, at least for Rachel, it was Brian's house.

Any properties that hadn't been burned in the street had been crushed and yet Mr Jameson came out of their house smiling and looking down at a scorched photo frame. It was a picture of the Jameson's and the McRacker's posing together in front of the band 'Navacross'.

He looked down at his wife. "Debbie, do you remember this, this was a great day and a sad one? I downloaded this from my phone and printed it off last year." He showed her the picture whilst she was packing a suitcase in the garden with the few remaining unburnt clothes she had salvaged.

She took the picture but looked up at her husband with the saddest of looks. "Do you think they're okay, do you think they'll come back? It's been days since they went there with the Dragons in hot pursuit, I mean what chance do they have against Dragons?"

Mr Jameson put his arm around her and his face took on a perplexed frown. "I'm pretty sure that we would know somehow if they weren't alive. If Rach could come home then definitely, she would, Sarah..." here he paused for a moment. "...Sarah became a child of that world and she is freer there than here. You know that I will miss her just as much as you do, if she decides to stay there."

Mrs Jameson just nodded and watched as a Black Limo rolled up and parked outside Brian's house next door.

Jack picked up a ragged football shirt out of the rubble that had been their home and studied it closely then said to Mary. "I don't think I'll be able to fix this thing this time, if Robin comes home, I think he might be angry with me?"

Mary looked at her husband in disbelief. "If he has been through what we went through when we were there, I think that football shirt will be the last thing he'll be worrying about don't you?"

Jack grinned at her. "It was a rollercoaster when we were there wasn't it, eh? Do you remember the Shriekers?"

Mary nodded. "Only too well Hubby O'mine and outrunning the Squelchers, they were disgusting!"

Grayson stepped out of the Limo with several agents as well as Regi's personal Aide. He surveyed the carnage all around. The folder he was holding was clearly marked 'Hero relocation'. Both families saw him and went to greet him. They all agreed that he had been one of the good guys in all this.

As they met, Grayson announced. "Good news Folks, we have bought a whole bunch of houses on the new Estate that can house everyone from the street. It's a temporary measure until your homes are all rebuilt."

Mrs Jameson smiled at him, he had been the only honest member of the establishment that they had known. "Thank you, Mr Grayson, we were wondering where we could go. Do you mean everyone here though? There's a lot of us."

Grayson smiled reassuringly. "Mrs Jameson, after what we have all witnessed and the sacrifice that your two daughters have made along with their very unusual friends, I think that the whole world is indebted to you and them. Rest assured that we will do everything in our power to make all of your lives a bit easier from now on. We have bought the whole of the new estate and can easily house you all there. Not only that but the Chinese Government have given you unlimited travel and tour guides at no cost. You must know how grateful the world is to you right now!"

Mary asked the awkward question that they had all wondered about. "So, what happened to Drake and 'The Minister' may we ask?"

Grayson looked at her sternly and then at the Minister's Aide, who simply looked away. "Mrs McRacker, Regi has had a few mental issues since your furry octopus friends engulfed him but oddly enough, he is a much happier person now, if somewhat childlike in his outlook. He is being well cared for! Seems like they had a, let's say, calming effect on him. I don't think he will be returning to Government any time soon though, presently he has to be spoon fed."

"And Drake, is he alive?"

Grayson looked at her for a moment. "I should say that is classified but actually, he is in a secure accommodation from which he will very likely never be released. Drake is too dangerous to be left roaming around in any world and is obviously quite unhinged as you all know. I don't think he will ever see the light of day as it were."

Mrs Jameson snorted much to her own surprise. "Quite rightly so! What about the Zoologist, Charlie, what happened to him?"

Grayson looked confused. "Ah yes, he is on secondment now at the North Pole, by the sounds of it he'll be there for a few years, probably quite a lot of years!"

Then it happened, the smell of vanilla wafted in the air, it was coming from Brian's Garden, just a tiny hint at first but then the wisp of smoke grew bigger and bigger swirling around in a circle. Mrs Jameson clutched her husband's arm and held her breath as several figures started to materialise from within the smoke.

Grayson signalled to his agents and they surround the area with guns raised and said to the families. "Just a precaution you understand." No one objected.

The first people to come through, to everyone's disbelief, were Kate, the Aide's brother and Mrs Mole. People were half expecting Kate but Mrs Mole! Everyone stared at the pony tailed warrior who had a bow strapped to her back, quiver of arrows strung to her waist, sporting a leather headband and with a dagger strapped to her thigh.

Mrs Mole strode straight past the gun wielding agents and hugged Mrs Jameson full on. Stepping back, she looked her straight in the eye. "Mrs Jameson, I owe you a huge apology, I once said that 'The apple doesn't fall far from the tree' and I now realise what a good thing that is. You must be an exceptional parent because your two daughters are, without doubt, exceptional. It has been a great privilege to be their Guides Leader!"

Mrs Jameson was stunned and stared at Mrs Mole wide eyed. Did this mean the girls were alive? "I don't know what to say Mrs Mole, ummm, do you still have the slippers, oh and thank you!"

Mrs Mole smiled. "This is a quick return trip for me so do

forgive, just came back to pick up my Bonsai. I have so missed it and I have an army of White Tigers to find a home for. I think Jack will know how tricky that might be and yes, those slippers are still so comfortable! Lovely to see you again though!"

Then she marched off to the remains of her house, to retrieve the small Acer from the front garden. She barely even noticed the decimated wreck of a house that she was once so proud of. She smiled broadly as she spotted that her little Acer had not only survived the recent carnage but even had a few new leaves beginning to sprout.

On seeing Kate and Regi's Aide, the agents all lowered their weapons. Pointing weapons at her hadn't gone too well for them the last time Kate appeared. She walked over to Grayson who nodded his approval of her. "Glad to see you back Kate but whether you work for us or don't now, I still need a debrief from you."

"Yes, of course Sir and no I don't think I shall be returning to the service."

Both of Regi's former Aides walked slowly to each other and just stood saying nothing for a moment. Then the first tried smiling, the effect was awkward to the second. "I am very pleased to see you brother, I have much to share with you." His voice trembling with emotion.

The second Aide also tried smiling and found it as difficult as the first. "I believe that we may require some time not being Aides, to discuss what we have experienced with others during this very strange time."

The Aides both straightened their ties at the same time. They smiled, the first ever genuine smile of joy that they had shared in their entire lives.

More figures appeared in the smoke. John came through first much to Mrs Jameson's annoyance and she let it show. "What have you done with Robin whoever you are and why were you trying to strangle my son? You just get yourself over here boy because…"

Robin appeared next, looking a tad roughed up, sporting three scars on his cheek and a properly ragged shirt. "It's okay mum, it's okay I'm here. I'm fine, this is John. He's okay I think, we're mates ain't that right mate?"

John smiled at his 'mate' "Yes Robin I think we are mates." Together they walked to the McRacker's gate.

Then two more figures appeared and Mrs Jameson beamed from ear to ear as both Sarah, sporting a sling and Rachel, covered in bruises, walked out of the smoke. She ran towards her girls and hugged them both to her with Mr Jameson not far behind. Mrs Jameson nearly broke her composure as her eyes welled up. "You came back Sarah, you came back! Oh! My girls you are hurt!" Almost overcome with joy she could barely get her words out.

Sarah grinned. "I had to come back Mum. I'm staying but the Minotaur gave me a gift. Look!" She pointed at her waist where a small child sized bucket hung from her hip, vibrated and let out a tiny wisp of smoke.

Jack quickly shoved the tattered football shirt behind him into his belt. He hugged Robin, this time, for the first time,

Robin hugged his Dad back, nearly knocking the wind out of him. "Son it's so good to see you, we have been so worried!"

Robin turned to his mother, who held her arms out in utter relief as Robin went to hug her. "It's been mad back there, Mum, Dad, I have so much to tell you and Dad…"

Jack looked expectantly at Robin. "Yes son?"

Robin smiled. "I saw the football shirt, it's okay, I am really looking forward to one of your hearty breakfasts."

Jack looked at Mary then back at Robin. "What, you mean now son? We um…" he started looking around the debris surrounding them.

Robin laughed. "No Dad, no! Tomorrow morning will be just fine!"

John looked around at the families. "Robin, mate, I've got to go, my Mum will be wondering where the hell I've been."

"Listen John, sorry if I was a bit of an idiot back there, for dragging you into all this but…"

John stopped him. "Don't be sorry mate! I'm alive, a bit surprised for sure after that journey but I wouldn't have changed a thing. You are an amazing kid and maybe my first ever proper mate, so thanks for being a mate, mate."

Robin took John by the hand and then embraced him saying into his ear. "You could write a book about this and probably make a few quid eh?"

John stood back from Robin and beamed. "Now you're getting the idea Kid. See you later, eh?"

Robin looked at his family, then over at Sarah. "Would it

be okay if I brought some people to see your show sometime?"

John laughed. "Free tickets for you guys for sure!" With that he nodded to Rachel, he smiled feeling bigger than he had ever felt before.

Robin's eyes twinkled mischievously as he said. "You sure bud, there's quite a lot of us, could make a dent in the profit margin?"

"Yes mate, free tickets for whoever you bring. By the way, I think my Mum would love to meet you people, see you later." Then he clasped Robin's hand and looked him straight in the eye. "It's been a blast mate. Thank you!"

Robin nodded. "I… we couldn't have done it without you John."

John nodded to Robin, the girls and the families. It was a nod of camaraderie with a smile, then he left wondering how he was going to explain all of this to his Mum. He knew though, she was going to love the fact that he had been where she had been!

Mrs Mole reappeared holding a pot with her Bonsai, smiled at the girls and said to Sarah. "I shall do my best to keep White Tiger on the right path for you Sarah. Have a great life girls, do try to stay out of trouble, for a while at least." Then winked at the girls and disappeared back into the smoke.

As she disappeared, a shout came from one of the workmen at the Jameson's house. "LOOK OUT!" A huge roof timber creaked then began to fall directly towards one of the other workmen. Kate instinctively flung out her arm, the timber stopped mid-air and the workman scrambled to safety out of its path. The families looked at Kate, Kate looked back at them and raised an eyebrow. "Interesting!" she said and smiled.

Just before the smoke faded altogether a small sticky projectile flew out of it and smacked Robin straight between the eyes with an audible splat. Everyone heard the faint but unmistakable sound of a Sprite sniggering, Robin shouted out in disbelief. "Kobalos!"

The End.

MAKE AN AUTHOR'S DAY!

If you enjoyed this book, a review would mean a lot. You can leave your review on Amazon here:

https://www.amazon.co.uk/gp/kindle/series/B099HDRK21

BOOKS BY D. J. CATTRELL

The Bucket Series

The Bucket

The Bag

The Impossible Challenge

The Box

And, for younger readers, *I Want a Hippo*

ABOUT THE AUTHOR

D J Cattrell is a Suffolk-based children's author who specialises in creating bespoke story workshops for schools. His middle-grade fantasy series, soon to release its final instalment, delights children up and down the country. He now also works closely with both Primary and Secondary Schools to deliver author visits, story workshops, and his fantastic 'Story Gift Scheme'.

Find out more about D J Cattrell via his website:
www.djcattrellauthor.com

www.ingramcontent.com/pod-product-compliance
Lightning Source LLC
Chambersburg PA
CBHW021145080526
44588CB00008B/226